I0839672

LOVE HAS DIFFERENT MEANINGS

BY: Tasheika S. Powell

Copyright© 2018

To my sister...

I firstly want to thank my Heavenly Father for giving me this talent; so that I could write this book.

I want to thank my mom, Afri Meikle for all of her encouragement that she gave in order to have this book finished.

I owe special gratitude to my sister, Shauntae Powell for having my back, rephrasing my sentences and just being there for me when I need moral and emotional support.

I want to thank all of my readers, motivators and basically just everybody.

Thank you all

-Tasheika Powell.

This book is about a young, attractive lady who is blinded by riches and material things while her sister is more of the nerdy type. Kaci met her dream guy, Dwayne Chisolm and got married but did she marry him out of love or for his wealth?

Is Dwayne really in love with this girl?

Will Kaci ever fall in love with Dwayne or will it be too late when she realizes that she is in love?

Let's read to find out more....

-Tasheika Powell

"Kaci, I don't want to scare mom and dad." Laci sighed as they left the Medical Complex.

"I already told you what to do." Kaci smiled.

"No, Kaci. I am not going to do that. I don't believe in using men for their money. But I am not telling mom and dad; and I don't want you to either."

"Like I care."

Three months after, while Laci and Shelly sat at a café.

"Laci, we need to go to the mall like now. When are you going to stop procrastinating?" Shelly asked.

"I just don't feel like going." Laci said.

"Laci, what's wrong with you? This is your sister's wedding and she is depending on you? Tonight is the engagement party and you have been putting off this shopping for the past two weeks now."

"Why can't I wear something that I already have in my closet? There is way too much spending going on for this fricking wedding!"

"Listen, I am your best friend and also your cousin and I know you too well. There is nothing in your closet to wear to this party. What are you planning to wear, jeans and sneakers?"

"You are right. I have nothing to wear. But guess what? I don't want to want to come to the party."

"Laci, you aren't the one spending the money. It's your sister's money. Spend it while you have it girl! Have fun once in a while! Let your hair loose!"

"Correction! You mean Dwayne's money! You of all person should know she's not in love with Dwayne, she is in love with his money!"

"Don't say that Laci! What do you know?"

"What do I know? Really? Kaci is my twin sister. I know Kaci inside out. She doesn't love Dwayne. He is rich and cute, Kaci loves that."

"How do you know that? Tell me, because it is obvious that you know something that I don't."

Laci sipped her coffee as she looked Shelly in the eyes.

"The day Kaci and Dwayne met, I was there. We went to the grocery store for mom, on our way from the airport after dropping dad there. As we entered H-F-B grocery store in Austin, this guy bumped into Kaci and his Sundae spilled on her blouse. She began quarreling as the guy tried to clean the mess off. She told him not to touch her and blah, blah, blah. Dwayne came along and told the guy that it was okay and that he'll handle it. She quarreled on Dwayne saying not because he is cute means that he could afford to get her blouse in a good condition. She made it clear that 'money talks' as her blouse was very expensive. Dwayne seemed to have gotten annoyed and walked away." Laci explained.

"But you still haven't gotten to the point?" Shelly responded as she bit a piece of her doughnut.

"If you'd let me finish then you would understand. As I was saying, Dwayne walked away and went towards his then Ferrari, he opened the door. Kaci's eyes glistened and she ran towards the car and before I even realize, we were all in the grocery store shopping together. Funny enough, Dwayne paid the bill and we went home with way more than we had planned to buy. Two weeks after, Dwayne was introduced as her boyfriend to mom."

"But that is love. You have to admit it that love comes in many ways and it also has different meanings. Laci, I am going to be honest; you are sounding very jealous. Did you want Dwayne to fall in love with you instead? Your sister is beautiful and sweet, Dwayne loves that."

"So I'm not beautiful?"

"I am not saying you aren't but you have to remember that you turn down every guy that comes your way."

"I just want someone who wants only me and someone who I can work with to achieve our goals. I don't want someone who was fed with a golden spoon all his life and doesn't know what to appreciate or how to. And to just let you know, Dwayne does not fall in that category. He is not my type so I wouldn't be jealous of their so-called relationship."

"Just be happy for your sister."

"I can't be happy for her when I know she is not in love with him. She is only using him. I'll go to the mall with you but I am not feeling the vibe for this party."

"Let's go."

"I just think everything is moving too fast. Not even six months since they met and a wedding is in process." Laci murmured.

"Stop the mumbling and let's go." Shelly said, as she got up from the table.

CHAPTER 2

Laci was twenty-one years of age and so was Kaci. Laci was of slim built, light in complexion, average height and has short straight black hair. She was a florist and was single. She wasn't the type of girl to dress up but would only throw on T-shirt and a pair of jeans with sneakers and go about her business. She enjoyed spending time at the library, reading and playing the piano at home whenever on her day off.

Kaci on the other hand was slim, tall, had long black shiny hair. She enjoyed partying, going out with her friends and going shopping. She had on two tattoos and quite a lot of piercings. She loved dressing up and she had a matching pair of shoes or slippers for every pants or dress she had. She had the look of a cover girl. She didn't work but depended on Laci, Damion and her parents and now Dwayne. Laci spoilt her because she loved her dearly.

Shelly was their cousin and also Laci's best friend; not that Laci had anything in common with her but she confided in Laci because Laci was reserved. She was twenty-two years of age. She loved going out and having a good time. She was a bank teller and she worked for what she wanted and believe in dating rich guys. She was currently engaged to guy from Florida.

All three girls grew up in Dripping Springs, Austin, Texas and still resided there with their parents and other families.

Laci and Shelly went to Barton Creek Square Mall and entered into Macy's. Laci sat on a chair and went on Facebook while Shelly was busy looking at dresses.

"Good afternoon, how may I help you?" A store clerk asked.

"Hi, my cousin here, is seeking a lovely dress for an engagement party tonight." Shelly smiled.

"What cousin?"

"Laci!" Shelly exclaimed as she realized that Laci wasn't with her.

"Yes!" Laci answered not even looking at Shelly.

Shelly grabbed the phone from her and threw it in her handbag. The store clerk laughed.

"What's that for?!" Laci shouted.

"We came here to shop for a dress well basically for you and you are on social media! Pick a dress you like!"

"I don't like any of these dresses."

“She is one of the fussy ones. No worries. We have some others of better quality over this side. Just follow me.” The store clerk said as she began to walk.

“Stop. She just hates dresses period. You would just be wasting your time. She is just blocking her mind from them. It’s just one night Laci, it won’t kill you.”

“I only promised to wear a dress on the wedding day. I didn’t plan for this.”

“Well you are going to wear this dress tonight. We are the bride’s family and we have to show ourselves appropriate in front of the groom’s family whom we are going to meet tonight. Come on Laci, don’t make it bad for Kaci. First impressions last.”

“So why should I pretend? I like jeans. So what?”

“This is a formal event.”

“We have dressing pants for ladies who prefer pants.” The store clerk suggested.

“Her sister ordered me to get her a dress. Can’t let the bride down.”

“I don’t want to buy anything.”

“I’m not going to argue with you. I like this dress. Can you take it down for me?”

“I don’t like pink!”

"Laci, I wasn't pointing on the pink dress. I was pointing on this black dress.
Thank you."

"It's too… I don't like it."

"Be quiet! It's not about what you like anymore. Go and try it on in the changing
room."

Laci grabbed the dress and stormed to the changing room. After five minutes Laci
came out in the dress. The store clerk smiled and gave her thumbs up. Laci looked
uncomfortable. Shelly jumped in front of her with a pair of black wedges.

"No! I am not wearing that!" Laci exclaimed.

"I didn't ask you anything. You can't wear sneakers with that dress." Shelly said.

"Why not?"

"You don't wear… Never mind, these are what you will be wearing."

The girls went to the cashier and paid for the dress and shoes. They left the mall
and went to the hairdresser.

CHAPTER 3

"Grace, tonight is the night! I can't wait!" Kaci smiled licking an ice-cream as they sat in Smoothies Paradise Yogurt, on Barton Creek Square Mall.

"I know girl! We can't wait! This rich guy who is cute and totally hot is all yours. Girl you are lucky!"

"I know right! I mean anything I want, I get. That's why I love him. His mom is super-hot. She spoils me more than Dwayne himself."

"Girrrrrrl! I want to find a man like that!"

"These men are so hard to find now a days. I am just lucky I found him! I'm blessed! Let's go and check these stores for a dress."

"But Dwayne isn't here."

"Grace, Dwayne isn't here but his credit card is."

"Kaci, you are blessed! He trusts you with his card and you guys aren't even married as yet."

"He trusts me very much. More than I even trust myself. He is so gorgeous! I want a dress that will put me in the spotlight tonight."

"Girl, you are already in the spotlight! You are engaged to America's second richest bachelor!"

The girls left the café and went into Forever 21 and bought an expensive dress after Kaci tried it. Grace bought a dress also. They then went into Claire's and bought a matching stilettos to go with the dress for Kaci. They entered Kay Jewelers and bought some gold jewelries to go with their outfits.

"Girl I have so much plans for this money." Kaci laughed as they left the jewelry store.

"Girl, Dwayne really loves you and you really love his money." Grace laughed.

"Don't let it look that way. Let's go to L'Amour Nails. I want Kym to do my nails."

"But we just did our nails the day before yesterday. Did you forget?"

"I want the glow in the dark nails. It's my night don't you think I deserve it?"

"Fine. Let's go. Kym looks like she is free."

"Kym!"

"I have been waiting on you girl!" Kym said drinking a box drink.

"I was shopping."

"So glow in the dark it is? Should I soak these off? Or just clean it off?"

"Just clean it off. I just want it to look pretty."

"Kaci, you are one lucky mother-fucker! Dwayne, the second richest bachelor, you are one fortunate bitch! Don't ever let anyone snatch him from you! Give him all the love you can!"

"Yup."

"You can even run the maid out of a job! Show him your cooking skills."

"Kaci? Show cooking skills? She'd have to attend cooking classes first!" Grace interrupted.

"You have a bitchy friend but you must love her." Kym laughed.

"Yeah, I love this bitch although she just spoilt my moment!"

"But seriously Kaci, you need to learn to cook. The way to a man's heart is through his stomach. That's how I got this ring."

"Cooking is not my thing! I already told him and he said he doesn't want a maid he has two already. He said he wants a wife."

"I got you girl."

"Whatever!" Grace smiled as she texted on her phone.

CHAPTER 4

At home, Mona and Patrick, the twin's parents, were busy as they decorated the outside of their four bedroom house at the back. The party was being held at their residence as they had come to an agreement with the other side of the family over the phone. Dwayne's parents had sent Kaci's parents a cheque to get the place in an appropriate order.

"Patrick, how does this look?" Mona asked.

"Honey, put it a little more to the left." Patrick stated.

"Mona!" Mrs. Singh called exiting the kitchen into the backyard.

"Yes mom." Mona answered sounding frustrated.

"Don't worry sweetheart. Everything's going to be okay. Uhmmm, I just took the last batch of cookies and cupcakes from the oven. I fried all the fish fillets, I made the kebabs and the salad. Damion and I are going to the grocery store to pick up the champagnes. Damion already called them. What's the name of the store to pick up the cakes? Is it on the same Mall?"

"Thanks mom. What would I do without you! Thanks a million! The cakes are at Great American Cookie Co.-I. It's the same Mall and ensure that the wines and champagnes are mixed. Please tell Damion to pick up his pants from Oakley's. The tailor called a few minutes ago. And mom please go into Great Wraps Grill and ask for Sandra and tell her I sent you for the Q fries I ordered and tell her to drop in some of the spicy sauces."

"Don't worry Mona, I am your mom and I am supposed to be here for you. All these places you are sending me to, are on the same Mall right?"

"Yes mom. Thank you so much."

"Mona, I love you and I love my grandchildren. This engagement party is going to turn out a success. I ensured I flew all the way from Puerto Rico to be here. So don't worry, your mama is here for you. Patrick is also here for you. Before I go, your father is watching the television inside, keep an eye on him. He is after the liquor."

"Mom, did dad really have to be here? You know he can be a disaster."

"Tawney will be picking him up when she leaves work."

"But Tawney promised Kaci she'll be at her party."

"Yes she'll be here. Tawney is taking him to her home, her husband isn't coming."

"Oh I see."

"Damion's calling me. I'll see you in about an hour."

"Bye mom. Patrick aren't you done yet? I am going inside to put up the balloons. Hurry and come help me. It's almost 3:00pm."

"I'll be there soon honey."

Mona went inside. Mr. Singh was still in the couch watching the television but he was eating some fruits. He was a grumpy old man. He was seventy-seven years of age and suffered from hypertension and diabetes.

"Dad! Why are you troubling the fruits?" Mona shouted.

"Can't I eat again? It's a problem to eat now!" Mr. Singh shouted.

"Dad stop it! Mommy just gave you something to eat! The fruits are too sweet for you! They were in syrup! And they are for the party! Can't you understand?"

"To hell with them being sweet! Everything is for the party! Party! Party! Party! What about your dad, the one who grew you? Don't I count?"

"Dad! Enough! It's obvious I care about you! The fruits are too sweet for you! You have diabetes! I always look out for you! You are just behaving obnoxious! The fruits are for your granddaughter's engagement party. It's for the guests!"

"So why the hell am I here if everything is for the guests?"

"I am done arguing with you!" Mona hissed as she continued putting up the balloons and decorations.

Mr. Singh sat mumbling to himself. Laci walked in. She was eating chocolate. Her hair had dropped curls and the end was fire red.

"Papa! What's wrong? Why the long face?" Laci said sitting beside him on the arm of the couch.

"Everything is for this party! Nothing is for me!"

"Oh no, Papa don't say that. That's not true. Everyone is just busy preparing for this stupid party but I promise everything will go back to normal after."

"You call it stupid?"

"Yes, it's quite a lot of money spending for two persons who barely know each other."

"But I want something to eat."

"I can't touch anything here but I promise you that I will take you to eat out tomorrow before you go back to Puerto Rico. I'll take you to a nice restaurant and you can eat all you want."

"That doesn't sound bad at all. I wish Kaci was like you. Damion is a good young chap. Kaci doesn't like spending time with me."

"Papa, I love your company. You are the world's best granddad. Whenever I get my leave I'll be done in Puerto Rico to party."

"I know you love Puerto Rico. It is your culture. You must love it."

"I'll treat you and grandma tomorrow. What do you say about that?"

"I have to see that happen first."

"You are a wise old man. I love you. I am going up to get ready. I'll see you later."

Laci walked towards her mother and began to help her.

CHAPTER 5

"Madame, your dress has arrived." Pablo the butler- of the Chisolm Mansion in Lakeway, Austin, Texas- said holding a dress bag in his hand.

"Finally, give it to me. Tonight is the night." Mrs. Chisolm smiled sipping her coffee before walking away.

Mrs. Chisolm was in her forties and was very hot. She looked very young and wore nothing below her knees. She had long curly brunette hair and always wore a pair of twenty-four carat gold wedding band on her finger. She was a fashionista. She owned a Saloon in Lakeway and a hotel which she partnered with her husband in Austin's square. She was very peculiar and liked things her way but was very down to earth.

"Margret! (Margret answered) Ensure that the gifts are finished wrapping and ready waiting on the table in the sitting room when I get down." Mrs. Chisolm said walking slowly upstairs.

"Mom! Which of these? This dress or this dress?" Chrystal asked.

"CC, when did you buy this? Didn't we go shopping yesterday?"

"Yes we did but I went out today and I fell in love with these two. I couldn't chose between either of them."

"You are just like me. Where did you buy them?"

"As they say like mother; like daughter. I bought them at Charlotte Rose on Round Rock Premium Outlets."

"I love Charlotte Rose's brands. I love the gold one. It goes perfectly with the shoes you bought yesterday."

"Mom, I hope the place isn't clustered. I hope their house is big. I am cluster-phobic."

"Since when? By the way, whatever the size of the house be it big or small, we will go there and enjoy ourselves."

"But mom, wouldn't it be better if we used the hotel lounge."

"For the wedding it can but for the engagement party, Kaci's place it is. She is going to be a part of this family very soon and her family needs to feel like a part."

"But mom…"

"Did I make myself clear? When you go, be on your best behaviour. Excuse me. I have a party to get dressed for."

Mrs. Chisolm continued upstairs. Chrystal stood on the stairs looking at her mother in a disgusted way.

Chrystal Chisolm was nineteen years of age. She was a Law college student. She was very boastful. She had long straight bleached hair which she coloured in purple with streaks of pink. She was slim, tall and very beautiful. She had the look of an innocent baby and her voice was soft. She loved shopping, even though she didn't wear half of the clothes that she bought as she easily changed her mind. She was an 'A' student and she loved partying a lot. She owned a swimwear line. She went upstairs into her bedroom.

Mrs. Chisolm went to have a shower and came out wrapped in a towel. She began to blow dry her hair. She then took up her phone. She made a call.

"Dwight, where are you? It's almost five and we have to be at Kaci's house by 6:30pm." Mrs. Chisolm said.

"Marsha, I am just leaving the office. I'll be there." Mr. Chisolm responded.

"Will you be on time Dwight? You are never early."

"I will be on time I promise. I am on my way. I am actually driving out now."

“Okay.”

Mrs. Chisolm continued to blow dry her hair before applying her makeup. Downstairs, Margret had just placed the gifts on the table and was returning to the kitchen.

“MARGRET!” Chrystal called out.

“Yes Chrystal?” Margret answered quickly.

“Where is my dinner?’

“I didn’t cook…”

“Why didn’t you cook?”

“Because Madame said…”

“Forget what Madame said! How dare you not cook!? What are you getting paid for?”

“But…”

“No buts! Prepare my dinner now!”

“Margret! Stop! I told Margret not to prepare anything and I heard her clearly stating that to you! We are going out and food will be provided there! Everyone will eat there and that is final!" Mrs. Chisolm said still wrapped in her towel at the top of the stairs.

"But mom, I don't know these people." Chrystal shouted.

"If you don't want to eat then tough luck! But Margret isn't going to prepare anything. Margret you can go to your room when you are ready. Chrystal don't be a spoil brat and go get dressed. We will be leaving soon."

"I am not travelling with you. Peter is coming to get me."

"Well whatever it is, I don't care! Go get dressed."

Mrs. Chisolm went back to her bedroom and closed the door. Chrystal stormed to her bedroom and slammed the door.

<u>*CHAPTER 6*</u>

"Hey dad! How are you?" Tawney smiled as walked through the kitchen planting a kiss on her father's cheek.

"Tawney, what are you doing here so early? The party hasn't started as yet. You are never early." Mr. Singh asked grumpily.

"Do I have to wait until the party has started to be here?"

"No baby, but you are really early. That is unlike you."

"It's my sister's house dad. What if I came to help out?"

"Dressed like that? My little girl doesn't dress like that for parties. I know you."

"Dad please. Hey mama!"

"Hey Tawney! Come and give your mama a hug. You are getting thick." Mrs. Singh said.

"No I am not. It's the work outfit. I need to go home and get dressed and you will see."

"Mona, isn't Tawney getting fat?"

"Just a little bit!" Mona laughed.

"Mona!" Tawney laughed.

"Ready to take him? I need to get him out before the guests start arriving." Mrs. Singh asked.

"Yes but he'll have to stay with Krissy and Kenardo's mom. Kenardo decided to come to the party after all."

"But you know he and that woman can't get along."

"Mom, you, dad and Mrs. Griffiths need to get a grip of yourselves. Kenardo and I have been together for like over ten years. This has to stop. Why can't you all act like civilized people? Anyways tonight they will learn. You are next."

"I hope they don't find the liquor."

"That's already taken care of. The liquor is locked away in our bedroom and no-one will have access to it."

"Good."

"You know what Kenardo and I plan to do one of these fine days?"

"What?"

"Close you, dad and Mrs. Griffiths in one room for the entire day with a bag of vegetable chips and a bottle of juice with three cups and one remote."

"Tawney, it's not that bad."

"You think so?"

"Yes mom it is that bad." Mona added.

"Yep, it is. Dad, let's go for a drive."

"I am coming! I am coming! We will be back in time for the party right?" Mr. Singh said as he kissed his wife.

"I will be not sure about you."

"What does that mean?"

"Never mind dad, let's go. Krissy is dying to see you."

Tawney and her father walked out of the house. She ensured that her father got in the car safely and got on the seatbelt before she closed the door and entered her side of the car.

It was now 6:15pm and Kaci had just pulled up the driveway in her black Mercedes Benz along with Grace. Grace took the bags from the car and followed her on to the porch. Kaci looked at the decorations which her parents had put at the front of the house and smiled before turning the knob to enter the house. The music blasted her ears. Some close friends and neighbors were inside. Kaci passed them all and went upstairs. She entered her bedroom and saw Laci sitting on her bed. She sat beside her. Grace sat on the window ledge as she placed the bags on Kaci's bed.

"Why aren't you dressed as yet?" Kaci asked.

"Nothing. I just don't feel like." Laci responded.

"Excuse me???? This is a special night for me and I don't want you to spoil it."

"Spoil it? How?"

"You are my twin sister. I know you. Don't think you are allowed to wear jeans. This is not high school Laci, this is the real world. You won't embarrass me like you did on Prom night. I won't tolerate it."

"I wore what I felt comfortable in."

"Don't do this to me Laci. I am begging you. Where is the dress you and Shelly bought today?"

"You know I don't wear dresses. So don't ask me anything about any dress."

"Laci please. No Jeans and no sneakers."

"I can't…"

"Don't worry Kaci. She won't. Here is the dress we bought. I'll ensure she wears it. Here is the shoes." Shelly interrupted as she entered the room.

"Wow! My sister has taste. I had no idea!"

Laci plopped down onto the bed with a loud moan. Kaci looked at the dress and tried on the shoes; as Grace and Shelly looked at Laci on the bed.

CHAPTER 7

"Mom! I'm leaving now! Peter's here!" Chrystal shouted.

"Okay! See you at the party!" Mrs. Chisolm shouted back from upstairs.

"Honey, how does this look?" Mr. Chisolm asked.

"Dwight. I already found this pink checkered tie to go with this blue shirt." Mrs. Chisolm said sounding upset as she grabbed the black tie and white shirt from Dwight's hand.

"Marsha, didn't it look okay?"

"Dwight! You wore black and white today. Can't you just wear pink and blue tonight?"

"Fine!"

"You take twice as much time as I do to get dressed. It's 6:30pm and do you have any idea where we should be by now? We don't even know where exactly we are going."

"It wasn't my fault. It was the traffic."

"Just hurry okay!"

Mrs. Chisolm had on a short straight pink and blue dress and her hair was caught in one with a messy bun. She had on a pair of hot pink platform shoes with her jewelries and her makeup was on point. She looked sophisticated. Her husband, Dwight had on a pair of black pants, a baby blue shirt with a pink checkered tie and a pair of black pointed shoes. They went downstairs. Mr. Chisolm went outside to get the car started as Mrs. Chisolm spoke to Margret and Pablo. She took up the three gift bags and walked through the door as Pablo closed it. They left at 6:53pm.

At the Robinson's house; the guests were arriving one by one. The music was moderate. Damion was outside instructing the guests on where to park and how. Mona had on a red floral dress knee length, a pair of black flat shoes and a pair of red earrings with a silver necklace and her wedding band. Her husband, Patrick, had on a pair of black pants, a white shirt and a pair of black shoes. Tawney arrived in a short black dress made from stretched material with a gold belt and a pair of gold stilettos with a gold clutch and her jewelries and makeup. She went upstairs to Kaci's room to leave her purse and phone.

Kenardo, Tawney's husband, had on a pair of black pants, a yellow shirt with the sleeves cuffed and a pair of black shoes. Almost everyone had a champagne glass in their hand. The upper class guests were now arriving. Mona and her mother were greeting the guests as they arrived inside and offering them champagne. Tawney was passing around finger food- kebabs- on a tray. Patrick's two sister were in the kitchen washing the items as they came in dirty. Chrystal refused everything that was being offered to her. She was disrespectful to Tawney. Tawney wanted to answer her but decided to be on her best behaviour and walked away. Her boyfriend, Peter took champagne and a kebab. He seemed to be enjoying himself.

"Chrystal, lighten up. You can't let the hosts feel this way." Peter said softly.

"It's tacky Peter. Who serves their own guests? Where are their caterers?" Chrystal smirked.

"CC, stop behaving so obnoxious. It's your brother's engagement party for god sake."

"I am just here because mom insisted. The entire thing is tacky. Right now I'd rather be at a club."

Mr. and Mrs. Chisolm arrived and went inside with a few of their acquaintances. They took their champagne and began to mingle with the guests. Mona and her mother stood looking at Mrs. Chisolm speculating if she was Dwayne's mother. Tawney was admiring her beauty.

CHAPTER 8

In the room upstairs. Kaci had on a long light pink dress which flushed her ankles, a pair of gold stilettos with gold jewelries and her silver engagement ring. Her makeup was on fleek. Grace had on a white off shoulder mini flair dress and a pair of pink stilettos with her jewelries. Shelly had on a very short blue dress, a pair of white stilettos and silver accessories. Laci sat on her bed in her sky blue flair dress. She had on a pair of sky blue earrings and a matching necklace and a little lip-gloss. It was now 7:30pm.

"Guys, go ahead. I want to talk to my sister." Kaci said closing the door as the girls left.

"Don't say it." Laci said.

"You know I am going to say it anyways. Get up put on your shoes and let' go. I don't want you to mess up my night. You always have a tendency to mess up anything I find special but I dare you not to tonight."

"I feel awkward."

"Laci, just do this for me please? I want you guys to make a good impression on his family tonight."

"So this is just about his family?"

"Laci don't go there. Tonight means a lot to me."

"Kaci why are you doing this? I know you don't love him."

"He's done a lot for me. He has given me experiences no one has ever gave me. He is spontaneous."

"Do you love him Kaci?"

"He taught me to drive, he bought me a car as a gift and he has done a lot for me."

"Do you love him Kaci?"

"He's a great guy. He's sweet, he's loving, caring, hardworking, generous and most of all he loves me."

"But do you love him?"

"Laci! It doesn't matter! He loves me and that's what matters."

"Why are you doing this? Mom and dad didn't raise us this way."

"I'm getting late. Let's go down."

"I hope what you are doing, is really worth it."

"I am not going to wait on a guy who I am in love with and who is in love with me and has money and all because it doesn't exist in this world. It is 7:47pm and I am going down."

Kaci left the room. She went downstairs. Laci sat on the bed. Kaci was surrounded by a few friends and she held a champagne glass in her hand. They were all laughing and talking softly. Kaci was extremely pretty. While standing and talking, she felt someone hugging her from behind. The person placed his head beside her neck and began to kiss her on the cheek. She smiled as he continued hugging her waist. Her friends snapped photos of them.

"Have I told you lately that you are very beautiful?" Dwayne whispered in her ear.

"No, you haven't." Kaci smiled.

"Really? So I have been a really bad boy lately then?"

"Is that supposed to be a question or should it be a statement?"

"What do you want it to be?"

"I think you already know your answer, Mr. Bad boy."

Dwayne laughed and turned her to face him. He kissed her gently on the lips and hugged her. She hugged him around his neck. Mona and her mother looked at them and smiled. Mrs. Chisolm looked at them and smiled along with a few more guests.

"You look so sweet. Never seen you dressed like this before." Kaci smiled.

"Well, you will be seeing many more, my love."

"Is that so, Dwayne?"

"Of course. After we are married and you help me get dressed in the mornings. You will."

"Why should I help you get dressed?"

"Because you will be the one taking them off in the first place. Just like how I want to rip this dress off you now."

"Oh Dwayne, you are so naughty."

"I am sure you love the naughty side of me."

"My lips are sealed."

"I love you."

“I know you do.”

Dwayne was dressed in a pair of well fitted black pants, an aqua blue shirt, a yellow bow tie and a pair of black shoes. He was twenty-four years of age. He was the Chief Executive Officer of one of his father's companies and was the owner of the golf club in his neighbourhood. He was tall, cute, light in complexion, had an athletic body and was super rich. He sported a Mohawk hairstyle.

CHAPTER 9

"Dwayne, honey." Mrs. Chisolm said touching him.

"Mom, you are here. I didn't see you." Dwayne said hugging her.

"Very beautiful Kaci. I love the dress." Mrs. Chisolm said hugging her.

"Thank you Mrs. Chisolm. You look fine yourself." Kaci smiled hugging her back.

"Kaci, I keep telling you to call me Marsha."

"Can I say mom?"

"That's even better."

"But I promise you, I'll call you that whenever you want me to but only after we live together, please?"

"No problem sweetheart. The decors are wonderful. The meal is awesome. I would like to meet a few of your family members now."

"Awwwww thank you. That's all because of mom and grandma. I'll go find them and we meet right there."

"Okay. I am going to find my husband and my daughter."

They walked away. Dwayne started talking to some other guests. Laci came downstairs and stood at the end of the stairs. She held a champagne glass in her hand. She felt awkward.

"Mom, come here." Kaci smiled.

"Look at my baby. You are so pretty." Mona smiled hugging her.

"Thanks mom. You are looking beautiful too, listen Uhmmm, you all are going to meet my in laws now so gather everyone and we are going to meet at the end of the stairs."

"Okay honey. Tawney, we are going to meet the family now. Kaci said we should meet at the stairs."

"Okay, I'll go call mom and Kenardo. They are outside." Tawney said putting some bottles on the counter before walking outside.

"Chrystal, we are going inside." Peter said.

"No. I am not coming." Chrystal resisted.

"Your mother just messaged me. We need to go and meet the other side of the family."

"(Sighs) okay. (Rolls eyes.)."

"Quit that attitude Chrystal!"

They walked inside. After ten minutes, they were all at the stairs. Laci was even more awkward. Dwayne and Kaci stood in the middle.

"You go first hon?" Dwayne said hugging Kaci.

"Okay, this is my lovely mom- Mona-, my dad- Patrick. This is my one and only brother, Damion. This is my aunt Tawney and her husband Kenardo. This cute chick here is my aunt Mel and her daughter Shelly. This is my grandma who flew all the way from Puerto Rico. You all know Grace my bestie. Last but not least this miserable baby here, is my other half, my twin sister Laci."

"Nice to meet you all. Laci I have heard a lot about you." Mrs. Chisolm smiled.

"Can this greeting and meeting get over with please?" Chrystal scoffed as everyone looked at her especially Tawney.

Dwayne took a deep sigh. Mrs. Chisolm shot Chrystal a dirty look.

"This is my splendid mom Marsha. My dad and my mentor Dwight. This is my miserable baby sister Chrystal and her boyfriend Peter. This is my cousin Steven and my aunt Patricia." Dwayne said.

Everyone greeted and the two mothers walked off together talking as if they knew each a long time ago. It was now 8:45pm and everyone seemed to be enjoying themselves. Laci was still at the stairs. Chrystal was standing outside, this time by herself as Peter decided to go and mingle with the guests. She was later joined by two of her cousins who had come outside. They each had a plate of food in their hand.

"Hi gorgeous." A guy dressed in a red shirt, a pair of black pants, a pair of black shoes and a black and red bow tie.

"Hi." Laci responded drily.

"I've been admiring you all night."

"And you are?"

"My bad, I am Kamari. And you are?"

"I am Laci."

"So why is such a beautiful girl like you standing here all by yourself?"

"Nothing."

"Not used to going out I guess. I can make you get acquainted with the guests here you know?"

"Excuse me! This is my house! I stand where I feel like!"

"I'm sorry. I had no idea."

"Why if a girl is reserved she considered as not being used to something! Guys like you disgust me! You all are too judgmental!"

"I am sorry."

"You can go and enjoy then party. I am not used to it."

"I am sorry."

The guy walked off looking very ashamed.

"Ladies and gentlemen! May I have your attention please?" Mrs. Chisolm said tapping her champagne glass.

After ten minutes everyone gathered.

"Good night everyone. I must say thank you for taking up our invitations to celebrate with us here tonight. Most of you know why we are here and some of you may be thinking that this is just one of my many gatherings. But tonight is a special night. Tonight most of us are in a different environment and setting. I hope you didn't get lost finding your way to our new location. I can just imagine that we are all enjoying ourselves. Mrs. Robinson and Mrs. Singh, the meal is awesome and thanks for the hospitality. Does everyone agree with me?" Mrs. Chisolm said before pausing.

There were sounds of cheers and tapping of glasses.

"Okay, tonight we are here to celebrate an experience that I hope we will all cherish. Dwayne and Kaci, come here please. These two angels met four months ago and my son fell in love with his soulmate. The moment I heard Dwayne talking about Kaci in everything he does I knew my son was in love, because he has never done this before. When I met Kaci, I fell in love with her immediately. She is such a sweetheart and she has a warm spirit and I know she loves my son (Laci looked at Kaci; Kaci looked at Laci) and they will make a happy team. I know I will soon have grand babies. (Everyone laughed) They can't stay a day without corresponding. Okay this has happened already but to make it official, I am letting you know, that Dwayne and Kaci are engaged."

There were sounds of cheers and tapping of glasses. Dwayne hugged Kaci and kissed her. Kaci barely hugged him back. Laci saw it all.

"One more thing, the wedding date is set. Dwayne and Kaci wants it to be legal before the year ends. So coming next month, December 20, 2016, Dwayne and Kaci will be tying the knot. Your invitations will be in your mailboxes by the day after tomorrow. Goodnight! Enjoy the rest of the party!"

Kaci pulled back.

"What's wrong babe?" Dwayne asked.

"Next month? When did I agree on that? I thought we agreed on next year March?" Kaci said angrily.

"What's the big deal?"

"Everything Dwayne! I didn't plan on getting married so soon. Why didn't you tell me you changed it? You promised me that I'll get married in March but obviously you don't keep your promises."

"I am sorry babe."

"Enjoy your party! Goodnight!"

Kaci walked off.

"Kaci!"

She went up the stairs. Laci watched her and smiled as she shook her head.

Dwayne stood at the stairs calling her. Laci walked over.

"Dwayne, do you want me to talk to her for you?" Laci asked touching him on his shoulder.

"Please do. Tell her I am sorry."

"Don't worry she will come around. I'll go talk to her."

CHAPTER 10

Laci walked up the stairs and entered the bedroom. Kaci was sitting on the window ledge crying. Laci removed her shoes and walked towards Kaci. She sat on her bed and touched her.

"Kaci, look at me." Laci said.

"What do you want Laci?" Kaci asked looking at her.

"It pains me when I see you cry. Plus you are ruining your makeup."

"I know…"

"Smile for me please… That's it I see it coming…"

"Laci, you know I love you right?"

"Kaci, no doubt about that. Tonight is supposed to be your night. You have always dreamed of this and now you are receiving it and you aren't enjoying it. Why are you crying?"

"I know this is a dream come through but Dwayne and I planned on getting married next year March and to my surprise I am getting married next month. I am the bride, why is this a surprise to me?"

"It's simple! He loves you and he wants to spend the rest of his life with you, the sooner you realize this the better you will feel. His mother loves you dearly and she is fond of you. I just hope you'll grow to love him the way he loves you. Or you can go downstairs right now and call this entire thing off."

"Are you crazy? I can't do that! I'll never get this opportunity in my life again."

"Well I don't know what to say. I just hope you'll grow to love him and stop using him."

"You will never understand Laci. He loves me and I love his money. That is the love."

"I just hope no one gets hurt in this scheme that you are plotting."

"Are you coming back down?"

"No. I am tired of these shoes."

"I guess those are mine now right?"

"You bet!"

"Okay."

Kaci went through the door and went downstairs. She spotted Dwayne but stayed clear of his course. She stood beside Grace and a few other of her friends as they congratulated her and admired her twenty-four carat silver diamond ring on her finger. The party ended around 12:30am. Chrystal was the first to leave at 9:37pm. Mr. and Mrs. Chisolm left at 1:09am after helping to clear the empty plates. Kenardo and Patrick were outside packing up the chairs and tables. Tawney and Mona were tidying the kitchen after they forced their mother to bed. Kaci went upstairs to bed. At the Chisolm's Mansion, Mr. and Mrs. Chisolm were in their bedroom around 1:46am, when Dwayne came in. He had a fierce look on his face.

"Sir, is everything alright?" Pablo asked.

"Chrystal! Chrystal!" Dwayne shouted ignoring Pablo.

The lights went on upstairs and his parents came out. Chrystal came out of her bedroom in her pink robe with a piece of burger in her hand and some fries, looking rather annoyed.

"Dwayne, what is this for in the middle of the night?" Mrs. Chisolm asked.

"CC, get down here now!" Dwayne shouted.

Chrystal went down.

"What's your problem?" Chrystal asked still eating her burger.

"How dare you! That's my girlfriend's place! My fiancé to be exact!"

"What did I do now?"

"Why the fuck were you there? Why did you even come there?"

"So all you had to do was tell me not to show up!"

"I am sick and tired of your dirty behaviour! Her family are such nice persons! They were very hospitable to each and every guests! Why were you being disrespectful to Kaci's aunt?"

"Listen, I had no idea it was her aunt okay? And did her aunt have to complain to you? I am sure it wasn't Kaci because she is not like that!"

"That gave you no right to be rude! How dare you tell Kaci's aunt that she looks like a slut when she was only being hospitable to you?"

"That was not hospitable enough!"

"God dammit! This was not a fucking five star hotel where it was expected that you got treated as a queen!"

"They could have done catering! That would have being a start!"

Dwayne slapped the burger from Chrystal's hand and it fell on the ground. Chrystal shoved him. Dwayne raised his hand to slap her and Mr. Chisolm was down in a flash. He held his hand.

"Don't you dare hit my daughter!" Mr. Chisolm shouted.

"Dwight! Let him go! Please remind your daughter that I had already warned her before we left!" Mrs. Chisolm shouted coming down the stairs.

"So you are taking his side? After he was about to hit your daughter!"

"Do you really want to argue with me, Dwight? I don't think so!" Mrs. Chisolm said hugging Dwayne around his waist and walking up the stairs.

<u>*CHAPTER 11*</u>

The following morning, Laci awoke and got dressed in a pair of black skinny jeans, a white blouse, and a pair of white sketchers and combed her hair in a ponytail. Just as she took up her bag and was about to leave the room, Kaci woke.

"Back to your old self again. Hmmmm." Kaci said sleepily.

"Good morning Kaci. I am more comfortable this way." Laci responded.

"Hmmmm. When will you ever change? Sometimes I am ashamed to call you my twin."

"Ashamed because I am not egotistic and materialistic like you? Because I believe in love for the inner person and not for wealth? Let me tell you this sis, I'd rather be hated for that even by you rather than be loved for wealth. I know you don't love him and the poor guy loves you so much."

"Correction! He is not poor; he is rich."

"Kaci when will you ever get it?"

"I just can't wait until the 20th of December so I can escape your annoying voice"

"If you don't love him, Kaci, don't marry him."

"If you don't like what I am doing. Don't come to my wedding."

"I am getting late for work."

Laci walked from the bedroom slamming the door behind her. She dried her tears. She began to go down the stairs.

"Laci, what's wrong with you?" Damion asked.

"Nothing. See you later." Laci sniffed.

"Wait! Let me drop at work. I am going up for my phone."

Laci continued down the stairs. Her mother was on the phone, as she buttered a slice of toast.

"… No Marsha, oh okay I understand… So I will meet you there in thirty minutes and we can chose the invitation package. Okay no problem. (Hangs up phone) Morning Laci." Mona smiled.

"Morning mom." Laci said.

"Why are you so down this morning?"

"Just a bit tired, that's all. Going somewhere?"

"I didn't see you much last night though and we needed the help."

"Mom please don't start."

"I am going to meet Marsha in Austin Square, to choose invitation packages."

"Marsha?"

"Where were you last night, Laci? Marsha is Dwayne's mom."

"Oh. But why do you have to choose invitation package? Don't one just get a simple invitation? This is all a waste of money mom, don't you think so?"

"Laci, this is your sister's wedding and her fiancé's family is in charge of the wedding so the least I can do as her mother is help them choose."

"Whatever."

"I think you need to focus on your life and find yourself a decent husband soon."

"Mom!"

"Yes Laci? I am serious! You need to stop meddling in your sister's personal life and get yours sorted out and stop turning these decent guys down. I understand that you are going to miss your sister but she will just be forty-five minutes away from you. You can always go and visit her. I know she is your companion but

Kaci has found her soulmate and she is ready to settle down, you need to slacken up a bit and let loose and find yourself a husband. You will be less miserable."

"Mommy how can you say that? You have no idea what is going on."

"What is going on?"

"Mom? Laci? You ladies ready?" Damion interrupted spinning his keys on his finger as he went through the kitchen door.

"Whatever mom!" Laci said going through the door.

At the Chisolm's Mansion, Dwayne was about to leave for work. He had on a pair of grey pants, a purple shirt with a purple and grey stripe tie and a pair of black shoes with his grey jacket in his hand. Mrs. Chisolm came downstairs in a purple pants suit with a white blouse under it and a pair of silver stilettos with a huge grey handbag and a file jacket.

"Pablo, come here." Dwayne said going towards the door.

"Yes Sir Dwayne." Pablo answered running towards him.

"I want you to send my jacket suits to dry cleaning today. I already laid the ones for dry cleaning on my bed."

"Okay Sir, not a problem."

"Dwayne?" Mrs. Chisolm called.

"Yes mom?" Dwayne answered turning around.

"For the wedding, what colour should I choose for your theme? Kaci is pink."

"Purple mom."

"Good. That's the colour I had in mind. Your wedding is going to be great!" Mrs. Chisolm said as they both walked through the door.

"Mom, do you think we are rushing it? I mean I really love Kaci mom, but I don't want to rush her."

"Did Kaci say something to you last night? You both were happy with the idea beforehand."

"I kind of didn't tell her mom. She was surprised last night. She still had March in her mind."

"You told me you had spoken to her. Why did you lie to me? I don't want to pressure this young lady."

"I was going to ask her and then I forgot. And when you ask me I just said yes."

"That's your fault mister. I already booked the officiator and my staff at the hotel are already preparing the lobby for the wedding."

"She was really upset with me last night."

"Fix it before she cancels! I can't lose so much money Dwayne!"
Mrs. Chisolm got in her car and drove out. Dwayne stood by his car with keys spinning on his finger. He had an extra cute look on his face. He took out his phone and dialed a number.

"Hello?" Kaci answered sleepily.

"Good morning babe." Dwayne smiled.

"Morning."

I guess you are still upset with me right?"

"What do you think, Dwayne?"

"I am sorry. I want to make it up to you. I want to show you how sorry I am."

"And how are you going to do that?"

"Come by my office today."

"Me? Your office? I am not coming there."

"Come on we are getting married next month. You have to know where my office is."

"But why do I have to come there?"

"Kaci do you love me?"

Kaci went silent.

"Well I know you do. You have all right not to answer. Such a silly question of me to ask. Just come by okay. I am looking forward to seeing you."

"Fine! I will! I am going back to finish my beauty rest. Goodbye."

"Okay. I love you."

"Yeah I know."

Dwayne drove out. Kaci pulled the sheets over her head.

CHAPTER 12

Mona arrived at Austin's square and waited on Marsha at the outside of Dragonfly Designs.

"Mona, I am so sorry for being late. I had to stop at the office." Marsha said.

"That's okay." Mona smiled.

"Let's go inside."

The two ladies went into the sophisticated building.

"Mona, how does this style look?" Marsha asked.

"It doesn't capture my attention." Mona responded.

"Really? It looks cute and rare to me."

"Marsha look at this one. It already has the diamonds and stars on it. We can get it customized right?"

"Mona, I love this! Why didn't I spot it before you? Excuse me. We have come to a conclusion. We are choosing this design."

"Okay Madame. Let me get the book." The sales clerk smiled bending under the counter.

"Pink and purple as decorations. The writings in silver and gold. Here's a picture of the bride and the groom. Dwayne Chisolm and Kaci-Ann Robinson cordially invites you to celebrate with them on December 20, 2016 at 2:00pm as they tie the knot, at Chisolm's Grande Hotel Auditorium, on Lakeway Avenue, Lakeway Neighbourhood, Austin TX 76549. Reception at 6:00pm in the Hall. R.S.V.P." Mrs. Chisolm said as the young lady wrote.

"Mrs. Chisolm, what colour envelopes?" the young lady asked.

"Mona, you choose."

"Silver and gold." Mona stated.

"Thank you. How many copies?"

"Seventy."

"Mrs. Chisolm and Mrs. Robinson, you can pick up the invitations in half an hour. Shawn get these printed and done now! It's express. The total is US$598.96."

"So much?" Mona asked.

"Mona it's express. And that price is nothing. It was expected."

"I am so sorry."

"That's okay. Now we are going next door. They have fine tastes in decorations."

"Okay let's go."

Kaci was now awake. She had a shower and did her makeup, after which she blew dried her hair and straightened it. She got dressed in a pair of white skinny jeans, a pink chemise blouse, silver jewelries, a pair of silver sandals and a pair of white shades. She took up her white handbag and cellphone and left the room. She went downstairs and saw her grandmother in the kitchen. She took up an apple and a banana and walked towards the door.

"Kaci, didn't you see me?" Mrs. Singh asked.

"Sorry. Good afternoon, grandma." Kaci said rolling her eyes with her back still turned.

"What's gotten into your head? Is it the wedding?"

"Nothing has gotten into my head."

"You knew if you were in Puerto Rico, you wouldn't be like this. I told your mother to send you girls back there. That fine young man really liked you. He would have made you a great husband. Because I know you don't love Dwayne."

"What was I going to do? Sell oranges in the market with him?"

"You both could have worked together. He was heartbroken when I told him that you were getting married to some rich guy here in Texas."

"I didn't want someone who sold oranges in the market for a living. He couldn't maintain me. Dwayne on the other hand gives me whatever I want."

"Do you really love Dwayne?"

"I have to go."

"Kaci-Ann I am talking to you!"

"I have an appointment. I'll talk to you later."

Kaci walked through the front door and left her grandmother standing in the kitchen with a dish towel in her hand as she shook her head.

CHAPTER 13

"Sir, may I come in?" Nicholas asked as he knocked the door.

"Yes Nick, come in. I was just about to call you." Dwayne responded seated around his desk on his desktop.

Nicholas entered and had a seat.

"Could you sign these for me please sir? They are the documents needed to get the transfer started."

"Send it off now. I need that transfer in my office tomorrow morning. And the cheques, what's happening to them?"

"I think Melissa has them sir."

"Get them from her. It should be one hundred and sixty of them. Tell Lennox to get them in envelopes and I need them before the day ends. I have to sort out the employees' files and so I can write their relevant bonuses on the cheques. I have to start distributing by next week."

"So early sir? Bonuses are normally given out a few days before Christmas."

"I know. But I won't be around. And I want to speak with each individual personally so I have to do it earlier. I won't around until sometime in January or so."

"Okay sir. I'll get to it right away."

"Good. Remember the transfer. (Puts receiver to his ear) Latoya did that certificate come as yet?"

"Yes sir. The courier just delivered it." Latoya responded.

"Get it to my office now. Put it in an envelope."

"Okay sir. Gerald, are you going upstairs? Take this and this to sir please? Sir Gerald is taking it to you along with some application letters."

"No problem."

At 12:49pm, Kaci entered the building. The air conditioner made her body shiver. She removed the sunglasses from her eyes placing it on her head as she approached the receptionist's desk. All eyes were fixed on her. She placed her hand with the engagement ring on the counter.

"Good afternoon miss, how may I help you?" Latoya asked.

"Where is Dwayne?" Kaci asked looking all around the office.

"Excuse me?"

"You heard me. Dwayne Chisolm?"

"Is he expecting you? Do you have an appointment?"

"Lady if I didn't I wouldn't be here asking for him."

"Let me call him first."

"No need to. Just show me his office."

"I can't do that. I love my job."

"Your job is safe. Just show me his office or else your job might be in jeopardy."

"Excuse me miss, you cannot speak to her like this. I would have to throw you out. She is merely doing her job." A young man said sternly.

"Do you know who I am?" Kaci asked rolling her eyes.

"It's obvious that we don't know you. Did you tell us who you are?" Latoya scoffed.

"Lady be extra careful how you talk to me."

"Hello sir, there is a young lady here to see you… She refuses to give us her name… Yes she is tall, slim and has a diamond ring on her finger. Silver sir. Okay." Latoya said hanging up the phone and looking at Kaci scornfully.

"What?" Kaci asked rather annoyed.

"Go straight up the hall, take a left turn, take the first stairs and continue to the third floor. His office is right in front of the stairs. His name is on the door. You can knock and wait to be acknowledged."

Kaci hissed her teeth and walked off. Four staff members crowded Latoya's desk and began speculating. They have never heard of Dwayne having a fiancé. Dwayne wasn't the type to have one female companion. Latoya called Dwayne's office in order to find out.

"Yes, oh I didn't remember, cancel it. I will deal with it next year. (Kaci entered the office without knocking) Don't worry, I'll call them. Have a seat babes. Latoya Uhmmm, I am busy now okay? Hold all my calls. Thanks." Dwayne said smiling at Kaci.

"I finally found it." Kaci smiled sitting down.

"You meant to say you finally decided to show up."

“Whatever.”

“You are looking wonderful today.”

“Aren’t I always beautiful?”

“Don’t say that babes. (Sits on the desk in front of her) I love you Kaci and I really want to spend the rest of my life with you. And I am so sorry about last night. I should have told you beforehand but I had a lot of work on my head. I am sorry.”

“I don’t know what to say to you Dwayne.”

“Maybe this will cheer you up.” Dwayne said handing her an envelope.

“What’s this?”

“You will only know if you open it.”

Kaci opened the envelope and took out the certificate.

“OMG! Baby! Thank you! Thank you! Thank you! You are the best!” Kaci screamed kissing Dwayne.

“You can use it this weekend. Do you know where the spa is?”

"I passed it twice a week when going to the gym. You definitely know how to make me feel special."

"Because I love you. You are my lady and it is my duty to spoil you."

"You are making blush too much."

"I want to feel special too."

"What do you have in mind?"

"What do you think?" Dwayne asked grabbing Kaci's ass and kissing her neck.

"Oooooooh, you are a naughty boy." Kaci smiled putting a love bite on Dwayne's neck.

"What do you say my place?"

"Okay, sounds good to me. I'll give you a wonderful massage."

"Let's go!" Dwayne smiled grabbing his jacket from his chair and slapping Kaci on her ass.

Dwayne opened the door and Kaci went out. He closed the door. He saw Nicholas in the hall way going to his office.

"Nick, I'll be out for the rest of the day. Get the transfer and the cheques on my desk. I need to see them by tomorrow when I return." Dwayne called out.

"Another one!" Nicholas grinned pointing at Kaci.

"She's special!" Dwayne smiled hugging Kaci.

Kaci looked at Dwayne and shot Nicholas a dirty and concerned look. Nicholas smiled and waved at her. Kaci hugged Dwayne and Nicholas saw her engagement ring. He was in awe. He couldn't believe his eyes. Kaci looked at him and smirked.

"I hear you, boss!" Nicholas smiled walking into his office.

Dwayne held Kaci's hand and they walked downstairs. When they got to the front desk he stopped. The workers quickly scattered from Latoya's desk as they were gossiping.

"Latoya, I'll be out for the rest of the day. Take my messages. Postpone all my meetings for this afternoon. Any emergency call my cell." Dwayne instructed.

"Yes sir." Latoya answered.

Dwayne hugged Kaci and they walked towards the door. The employees began looking at them.

"Do you want something to eat?" Dwayne asked as they went towards the parking lot.

"Yes. I only ate a banana and an apple this morning." Kaci smiled.

"Okay, what do you want?"

"I haven't ate KFC in months."

"Okay meet me there."

"Okay."

They both went towards their own vehicles and drove off. Dwayne followed Kaci.

CHAPTER 14

"Mona, the decorations are taken care of and the invitations are with us. You know what I want you to do?" Mrs. Chisolm asked.

"What's that?" Mona asked.

"The bakery that you bought the engagement party cakes from, do they cater wedding cakes?"

"I think so. You want us to go there? It's just down the street."

"Let us go. Mona I want you to be a part of this wedding. I might be spending the money but I need your ideas."

"You are so sincere."

"Let me tell you something, a lot of persons don't think I understand the struggles of life because of my social status. I am not just down to earth because I want to. I am this way because I am from a poor background. My father sold in the market and my mother was just a housewife who sewed now and then. I didn't really go to school. There were six of us RIP to my brother, and we had to take turns going to school. We lived in Puerto Rico."

"Where in Puerto Rico?"

"The beautiful city of La Perla."

"Really? I am from Old San Juan!"

"So we were practically neighbours."

"I can't believe. This is fantastic news."

"Well as I was saying, I was one of the three students who got scholarship for The University of Texas at Austin, there it is right over there. My dad sold his tractor and some other tools to pay my fare and all. I didn't want to go but my parents believed in this line 'God Will Provide'. They lived on nothing. Being a freshman, Dwight was a senior and boy did I like him but he was out of my league. I got a part time job at a small café in town but guess what?"

"What?"

"Dwight frequented that café. And each time saw him I got weak in the knees. He was super cute not saying he isn't now but he had many girlfriends and I didn't knew he liked me too and that's why he frequented my workplace. One day I was at work and I went to the back and started smoking and broke down into tears."

"Why?"

"(Sobs) my father had passed away the day before. I was on my third year and I had exams to pay for. The scholarship only lasted for two years. My rent was overdue and I wasn't working enough. I sat right in the back and planned my suicide. My mom was unemployed and two of my sisters had babies with no fathers, one was sixteen and the other was thirteen and the others three ranged from four to nine. I just couldn't go on anymore."

"Stop the crying. Please?"

"A lady happened to pass by and saw me. I don't know what she was doing there she was too fine to be there; but I felt comfortable with her. It was like I knew her long ago. I poured out my heart to her. She's and will always be my confidant. May her soul rest in peace. She took me into her home. She paid for my exams and sent money back home to mom."

"Wow! She is an angel!"

"Yes she is. And guess what, she turned out to be Dwight's mom. We started to go out secretly because she warned him not to look at me but I loved him and he loved me too. She eventually found out when I was eighteen, a year later and we got married when I was nineteen. Dwight was twenty-five and I became Mrs. Chisolm, the wife of the now business tycoon. I worked for what I wanted and I got what I deserved. The moral of my story is to never forget where you are coming from. I only share my story with those I am fond of.”

“That’s so sad. I am so sorry and I am happy for you at the same time.”

“I know right. I just want Kaci-Ann to always remember where she is coming from. I don’t want her to forget her roots because she is marrying my son.”

“She won’t forget. I know all my children well. She loves your son very much.”

“I know she does. She has changed my son also. He wasn’t the responsible type, but since the last four months I have a changed son. Enough of my drama. Let me dry my tears and let’s drive.”

“Your story means a lot to me.”

CHAPTER 15

Two weeks later.

"MOM! LACI DOESN'T WANT TO GO DRESS FITTING!" Kaci shouted storming from upstairs.

"Laci! We need to go! Tawney and Shelly are waiting! And we have to go pick up Grace and Sabrina!" Mona shouted from the kitchen.

"And my in laws are waiting also!"

"Fine! Why do I have to wear this stupid dress anyways?" Laci muttered coming down the stairs.

"Because you are my maid of honor!" Kaci said rolling her eyes.

"Why didn't you allow Grace or Sabrina to be your maid of honor?"

"Because you are my fucking sister! I just want my sister to be there with me! Ugh! You are officially the worst fucking twin sister one could ever have!"

"Kaci-Ann! I am standing right here and you are defiling your sister like that! You know your sister has a phobia for dresses. And Laci-Ana, you are doing this for your sister. It's just one day. The dress isn't going to strangle you. Now let us

go. Marsha and the other ladies are waiting on us. Kaci-Ann and Laci-Ana fix

your faces now."

Laci rolled her eyes. Kaci got in the driver's seat, Laci went in the back and Mona

went in the front. They left. They fetched Grace and Sabrina. They arrived at the

bridal shop at 11:15am.

"Sir, why did we receive our bonuses so early?" Latoya asked, while she was in

his office drinking coffee.

"I won't be around. I will be out by next week. Won't be back until about

February I guess." Dwayne smiled looking out the window.

Dwayne's phone was on the desk. Latoya looked at it and saw Kaci's photo being

the wallpaper. She frowned.

"Going on vacation?"

"Yes. I need some time for myself. Nick's in charge (cell phone rings) hold on,

hello? Oh crap! I totally forgot! How could I forget the rehearsal? Where is Kaci?

I'll be there by 12:30pm. Oh yeah I think Kaci is with mom, they are supposed to

be trying their dresses today. See you at 12:30pm. Back to you… All major

meetings should be scheduled for any time after February. Nicholas will manage everything else. I already had a meeting with him. What am I forgetting?" Dwayne said as he sat in his office chair clicking his pen.

Latoya began biting her nails and looked at Dwayne seductively.

"Sir, why is that girl (sighs) frequently visiting this office? You know I don't like it. I hate when other ladies come here to you and then you leave with them. But this girl has no manners and I would like if she stops coming here."

"Latoya, what we had was history and you know that. We ended that like six months ago. By the way what we had wasn't serious. It was just a fling. We were both conscientious of that."

"But sir, I still have feelings for you. She is coming around way too often now. It is very irritating! And she is your wallpaper on phone! This is getting out of hand Dwayne!"

"Listen to me and listen well. That girl's name is Kaci-Ann and you are going to respect her. She is my fiancé and she holds a very prestigious position that you could not hold. We are getting married and soon she will be your boss' wife and she can fire you. So if I were you I'd get my acts together."

Fiancé?! You didn't tell me you were, I don't even know what to say! You told me that you would never get married so what is gotten into you Dwayne!"

"I DON'T NEED TO EXPLAIN MY LOVE LIFE AND MY EVERY MOVE TO YOU! YOU ARE MY RECEPTIONIST AND NOTHING MORE! GET THAT THROUGH YOUR THICK SKULL! I WOULD NEVER GET MARRIED TO A WOMAN WHO SLEEPS WITH ALMOST EVERY MEN IN THIS ESTABLISHMENT! I THINK I AM FINISHED WITH YOU! YOU MAY LEAVE!"

Latoya hurriedly left the office crying with her notebook. Dwayne took a deep breath as he hissed his teeth. He grabbed his jacket from his chair and left the office. He ran down the stairs.

"Latoya I am not in. transfer all calls to Nick!" Dwayne said walking from the building as Latoya looked at him and recalled the moment in the office.

CHAPTER 16

The day of the wedding. The auditorium was beautifully decorated in pink, purple, gold and silver. There were securities at the entrance collecting invitations and ushers, ushering the guests to their seats.

Dwayne stood in front of the mirror. Looking back at him was a tall, handsome young chap; dressed in a white and gold tuxedo with a shocking purple shirt and a white and gold bow tie with a pair of white and gold dressing shoes. He was looking dapper. His best man had on a pair of black pants, a purple shirt with a gold vest and a pair of black shoes. His four groomsmen had on purple shirts with pink bow ties, black dressing shoes and black pants along with the ring bearer. The photographer took pictures of them.

"Dwayne, how are you feeling?" Shane asked.

"Bro, I am nervous. I literally have cold feet." Dwayne laughed.

"That's the norm. Now if you didn't then I'd be scared. Every groom feels this way before the wedding."

"Suppose she doesn't turn up at the altar?"

"D, I felt that way too three years ago but Nicole did turn up; don't worry man. Kaci loves you. If she didn't she wouldn't agree to this marriage."

"Shane what if she has cold feet?"

"Dwayne, it is normal. Kaci is not like those girls you had a fling with. She is not like your receptionist. She is an angel that fell from the skies."

"Dwayne, my son! Looking sharp today my boy!" Dwight said patting Dwayne on his shoulder.

"Ahhh dad, don't I always look sharp?" Dwayne asked.

"Not saying that but today you are a little extra sharp."

"Excuse me? May I have a father and groom photo please?" the photographer asked.

The groomsmen gathered to take pictures some funny and some serious.

A few rooms away, the ladies were all laughing and talking. Their makeups were already done. Kaci's makeup was on fleek. She was in a chemise dress. They were all playing pillow fights except for Laci who was in a corner all by herself on Facebook and Instagram. After half an hour they began to get dress. The hairstylist was doing Kaci's hair. The four bridesmaids had on short flair pink dresses with purple bouquets and gold stilettos. Laci being the maid of honor had on a long silky pink dress with her purple bouquet and a pair of pink sneakers. Kaci was still in her robe. It was now 1:57pm.

"Laci, you cannot wear sneakers! Why are you doing this to me?" Kaci quarreled.

"I am not wearing those!" Laci shouted.

"You have to! I am calling mom!"

"No matter what you do I am not going to wear it!"

"Wear these." Chrystal said handing her a pair of pink wedged shoes.

"No!" Laci shouted.

"They are more comfortable than the stilettos. Don't do this to your sister on her wedding day. Please?" Shelly begged.

"No!"

"Laci, the sneakers don't look appropriate with this attire." Sabrina said.

"Uhmmm ladies I can run to the store and get a longer dress to suit her?" the hairstylist asked.

"Please do. I don't want my sister in law to be embarrassed on this day." Chrystal said.

Just then Tawney's daughter entered. She was six years of age. She had on a short white dress with a basket filled with flowers. Everyone crowded her except for Kaci who was quarreling on Laci.

"Ladies?" Mrs. Chisolm said, entering the room.

"Yes." They answered in a chorus.

"Kaci, you still aren't ready?"

"My makeup got smudge so I am reapplying it." Kaci smiled as the makeup artiste applied the makeup.

"My poor baby has to wait so long."

"I'll be ready in the next half an hour."

"You all are so beautiful. See you all in a bit. Hello? What? I am coming? Excuse me ladies, duty calls…"

"What do you mean by duty calls?" Kaci asked looking worried.

"Nothing to worry about. I am just going to settle a query with a paying guest. That's all. I'll see you in a bit."

About 2:36pm, Kaci was standing in front of the mirror, reflecting back on her was sweet, fierce girl. She had on an extravagant white Cinderella wedding gown with silver studs with a white veil lined with gold and a pair of gold stilettos with her initials printed in silver on the bottom. She held a pink and purple bouquet in her hand. The photographer snapped a few photos. At 2:47pm they all walked from the room. She hugged her father.

"You look beautiful honey." Patrick smiled.

"Thanks dad." Kaci smiled.

"Looking like a princess." Mona smiled.

"Mom, stop the crying."

"I am going to miss you tormenting your sister. The house is going to be different without you."

"Mom, don't. Can we go in before I change my mind please?"

The flower girl marched inside sprinkling the flowers as the photographer snapped photos and the videographer videoed. The bridesmaids marched in next followed by the maid of honor, Laci. Everyone turned to look at Kaci as she marched down the aisle with her parents.

Throughout the ceremony.

"The Bride and the Groom have personalized vows. So we won't go the traditional way, Dwayne you may go first." The officiator said.

"Here goes." Dwayne sniffed.

Everyone laughed.

"Today surrounded by a lot of eyes of people who love us as much as I love you, I choose you Kaci-Ann to be my life partner. I am proud to be your husband and to join my life with yours. I vow to support you, push you, inspire you and above all love you, for better or worse, in sickness and health, for richer or poorer as long as we both shall live." Dwayne read afterwards hearing a series of awes in the audience.

"And now you Kaci-Ann." The officiator repeated as Kaci took a piece of paper from Laci (Laci had written the vow)

Kaci shot Laci a dirty look as she mumbled to herself. Laci smiled.

"In the presence of God and these our family and friends, I take thee to be my beloved, promising with divine assistance to be unto thee a loving and faithful spouse so long as we both shall live." Kaci read.

"Kaci-Ann you sounded very nervous. With that said, I now pronounce you man and wife, you may kiss your bride." The officiator said as Dwayne kissed Kaci.

After the wedding they left for their honeymoon in Jamaica.

CHAPTER 17

They returned home the twentieth of January.

"Welcome to your new home." Dwayne smiled as he lifted Kaci and brought her upstairs.

"You didn't have to." Kaci sighed.

"Why not. I cannot take my hands off you for not even a second."

"Hmmm."

Kaci unpacked her clothes and rearranged some of the items in the room. Dwayne sat watching her.

"Kaci come here." Dwayne called.

"Yes?" Kaci responded.

"These are yours."

"Are you serious?!"

"Yes, it's all yours."

“OMG! My own MasterCard, this is a Visa card, an American Express and two Platinum Cards. Thank you baby!” Kaci screamed kissing Dwayne.

“That’s not all. I am making you the CEO of my Golf Club which consists of a gym!”

“You didn’t have to!”

“Of course I have to. You are my wife and everything I have is yours. I’ll pay your credit card bills at the end of each month and I opened a joint account for the both of us. Tomorrow at 1:00pm we are going to the bank to sign your name and now you are the CEO’s wife so you know what that means?”

“I can hire and fire.”

“Yes but be tactful.”

“I don’t really want to do that though. Do I really have to do this? I mean all these things?”

“Take your time to adjust. I am not rushing you. But I know you won’t take time to adjust with the cards because of the bill I received last month.”

“Whatever.”

Four days after, Dwayne was going back to work. He awoke beside Kaci who was on social media. It was now 7:16am.

"Good morning beautiful." Dwayne said trying to kiss Kaci as he tried fingering her under the sheets.

"Morning. Stop! Didn't you get enough on our honeymoon?" Kaci hissed as she pushed Dwayne away.

"What's that supposed to mean? I am your husband and we are newlyweds."

"The whole fucking world knows that! And you being my husband doesn't mean that you own and can fuck me whenever you want!"

"Kaci! What's wrong?"

"Aren't you supposed to be going to work?"

"Did I do something to offend you? I am sorry for assaulting you!"

"(Hisses teeth) Excuse me!" Kaci said getting out of bed grabbing her robe from a stand.

Dwayne rolled over the bed and grabbed her hand.

"Ouch! You're hurting me!" Kaci cried.

"It was meant to. What is going on Kaci?" Dwayne asked sternly.

"Let me go! My hand!"

"(Sighs) go ahead."

Dwayne laid on the bed looking at Kaci as she put on her robe. She opened the door and left. She went downstairs into the kitchen and was given coffee by Margret. She sat on a stool by the counter snapping on snapchat.

"Madame Kaci, what should I get you for breakfast?" Margret asked.

"Scrambled eggs and toasts." Kaci said drily as she sipped her coffee.

"Good morning sis!" Chrystal screamed hugging Kaci.

"Good morning sweetie!" Kaci replied hugging her and kissing her on the cheek.

Chrystal sat on a stool in front of her and ordered her breakfast.

"How are you? Haven't seen you since you guys got back which is not fair. I am jealous of you guys! You are always on the road together! So my time! Are you okay?"

"Yes I am okay and how about you?"

"Yes I am okay. Have exams today."

"What kind of exam?"

"Law Basics! God help me!"

"Oh okay I know nothing about law but you are going to do great!"

"You think so? Being a criminal lawyer is not easy!"

"You will. I have that much confidence in you."

"You know that you are the perfect sister that I never had."

"Thanks to me!" Dwayne interrupted hugging Kaci from behind and kissing her.

Kaci frowned.

"Yeah, thanks to your bro, who got me here." Kaci said forcing a smile.

"I just love seeing you both together. You are such a cute couple!" Chrystal smiled snapping a pic of them.

"I know right." Kaci said walking off and headed upstairs.

"Madame! Here is your breakfast!" Margret called out.

"Just cover it. I'll get her back down here." Dwayne said running up the stairs.

Chrystal shrugged her shoulders as she had her cereal. She left the house soon after.

"Kaci, which of these ties should I wear with this yellow shirt?" Dwayne said holding up a yellow plaid tie and a black tie.

"I didn't get married to you, to dress you! Not because I am your wife means I am obliged to do so!" Kaci hissed texting Grace.

"Babe, I just wanted your opinion."

"Just wear something!"

"I don't know what the fuck has gotten into you!" Dwayne hissed and walked from the room slamming the door behind him.

In the afternoon, Kaci got dressed in a yellow flair dress, a pair of yellow wedged slippers, white accessories and a white bag. She left the house and met up with Grace and Sabrina. They met at Village Square Plaza in Lakeway inside of Café Lago to drink latte and eat freshly baked blueberry muffins.

"Hey girlfriend!" Grace said getting up to kiss her.

"Look how she is glowing!" Sabrina laughed.

"Hey my babies! Did you guys miss me?" Kaci laughed.

"To heck we did! But you have a new life now!" Sabrina smiled.

"No! I hate it!" Kaci sighed eating a piece of muffin.

"Why? You have been married for like one month." Grace asked.

"Dwayne is annoying! I can't stand him! Every morning he wants to kiss like do I look like a kiss cake or something?" Kaci snapped.

"Kaci, he is your husband. He is obliged to do that. I am not married and I would die if Kevin doesn't kiss me in the mornings." Sabrina smiled.

"You don't understand. I am tired of Dwayne." Kaci sighed.

"Tired? Don't tell me you only got married to Dwayne for his money?" Grace asked.

"I don't love him. I love the gifts. Speaking of that I got five credit cards and I am now the CEO of his Golf Club which I have no fucking idea about!" Kaci laughed as her friends looked at her seriously.

"Kaci, you did business in school and also management. You darn well know the role of a CEO! And try not change the subject. Why did you get married to Dwayne?" Grace snapped.

"I don't know. He loves me though. But he is annoying. This morning he wanted me to choose ties for him. Like what the fuck does he take me for?" Kaci argued.

"Kaci, you are his wife! That's a part of your duty being a wife!" Sabrina snapped.

"Kaci, you have only been married for a month and four days. You can't be pushing the man away so soon." Grace sighed.

"You guys don't understand. I didn't love Dwayne. I love the gifts and the money. Now I am married they all belong to me but I didn't sign up for wife duties!" Kaci scoffed.

"I hope you will love him soon before it's too late." Sabrina said.

"I can't believe you Kaci. I didn't expect this from you. Sabrina I think our lunch break will be expired in the next twenty minutes. We have to drive back to Austin." Grace said.

"I'll take care of the bill. Waiter!" Kaci called.

Grace and Sabrina hugged and kissed her and then left. She sat looking at them as they exited the café. She paid the waiter and tipped him before leaving. She drove to Austin square and went on Barton Creek Square Mall to shop. She then went to do her hair and nails. She arrived home at 7:47pm with her shopping bags.

"Baby where were you?" Dwayne asked as she entered the bedroom.

"Do I have to explain to you my whereabouts now?" Kaci snapped throwing the bags on the bed as she took off her shoes.

"I have been calling your phone and went to voicemail. I had to lie to my mother that you went out with friends."

"So what? I am an adult. I don't need to consult you before I go anywhere!"

"I am you husband and you need to communicate with me."

"I am tired and I am not in the mood tonight. So I am going to have a shower and go to bed. I don't want to be disturbed."

Dwayne went after her but she slammed the bathroom door in his face.

CHAPTER 18

Two months later and the relationship between Dwayne and Kaci wasn't any better. Dwayne was trying really hard to make his marriage work. Kaci only wanted to party night after night and go shopping. Dwayne couldn't touch her unless they were around the family members.

"Baby we have only been married for three months and we fight every day. You make me wonder if I really made the right decision in getting married to you. Maybe I should have just played you like the fucking game you are. Chad was right, I was moving way too fast! Kaci I am talking to you!" Dwayne cried as he sat on the bed and Kaci applied her makeup.

"Dwayne I am tired okay. Stop the crying. Be a man." Kaci sighed as she dropped the towel revealing her underwear.

"That's the best advice you have to offer me? Where is the Kaci I met last year? That sweet girl I could talk to about anything?"

"Speak to Chad. He's your best friend."

"Kaci we need counselling."

"I don't need any counselling. I had a long night and I have a meeting this morning so please don't get on my nerves."

"All you do is party and shop! What about me, your husband? I have needs too! When was the last time we had sex? I am married and I can't touch my wife! I have to be pretending that everything is okay! Kaci! The last time we had sex was on our honeymoon! You need to do better!"

"So sex is what is making you mad! Okay I'll fuck you tonight since you are lacking sex or do you it now before you go to office!?"

An argument developed. Chrystal sat in her bedroom hearing everything. She went downstairs.

"Mom! Dwayne and Kaci are fighting again!" Chrystal said to her mother in the kitchen.

"Stop eavesdropping on them. I am tired to tell you that. They are probably making love." Mrs. Chisolm smiled taking up her handbag.

"Mom, it's not the first! I keep telling you that they quarrel every day! It's not even 8:00am and they are fighting now."

"CC, I said it's probably nothing. They are adults and you young people tend to have sex in a particular manner and they look like one of those couples."

"You don't understand, don't you? Can't you see that your son is hurting? He is your favourite and you don't see it. They are only pretending when they are around us. I am a lawyer and I can pick these things up."

"CC, I am warning you for the last time to get out of their personal life."

"Mom, my brother is hurting. Kaci doesn't love him. If you won't do anything about it, I will."

"Honey, they are a married couple. Quarrels are normal and fights too. That happens between your dad and I quite often and that doesn't mean we don't love each other."

"You don't understand mom. Even Margret and Pablo know. I hear them talking. Dad is hardly here so he wouldn't know and you… You are clueless."

Just them Dwayne stormed downstairs. He was huffing and puffing.

"That is what you have done!" Kaci shouted slamming the door.

"Dwayne!" Mrs. Chisolm called out.

"Not now mom!" Dwayne shouted going through the door.

"I told you. I am going to his office. I have to get to the bottom of this." Chrystal said.

"No! Leave personal affairs at home!"

"No mom. I won't listen to you this morning. I need to help my brother. Kaci is hurting him."

"Kaci!" Mrs. Chisolm called.

"Don't call me! You and Chrystal can continue talking about me behind my back! I don't want to hear it!" Kaci said going through the door.

Chrystal looked at her mother whose mouth was wide open. She left. Mrs. Chisolm left afterwards.

"Sir, Mr….." Latoya started but Dwayne just walked pass her.

Everyone stood looking at him. About ten minutes after, Chrystal walked in briskly. She passed the staff and went upstairs. When she entered the office she saw Dwayne looking out the window and sniffing with his hands in his pocket.

"Dwayne?" Chrystal called.

“Sis, what are you doing here?” Dwayne asked turning around.

“What is going on between you and Kaci?”

“I don’t know. I really don’t know.”

“I know you guys aren’t happy. I hear you both every day. I sleep with it and I wake with it. I even study with it.”

“Where did I go wrong, CC?”

“Bro, you haven’t done anything wrong. You love Kaci with all your heart and she just needs to do her part.”

“So you know everything?”

“Yes, I am actually using it as a practical for school. Just give her some space.”
“SPACE!!!!”

“Don’t you shout at me. I don’t know what else to suggest but please can you calm down. Will you do that for me?”

“I’ll try.”

“And we are going out tonight.”

“I guess I can't say no?”

“You know you can't. We are going to party. I love you.”

“I love you too.”

Chrystal left the office.

CHAPTER 19

"Latoya?" Chrystal said.

"Yes miss." Latoya answered.

"Get Dwayne a cup of tea and some crackers please and minimize his disturbance today."

"Okay miss."

"Nicholas, come here."

"Yes miss?" Nicholas answered.

"Cancel Dwayne's meetings today but if you can head it without his intervention do it. He is in office but I don't want anyone to disturb him. Any major details call me or his wife but she's not in a good mood so call only me. Don't pressure him today please." Chrystal instructed.

"Okay. Miss Chisolm, the Uhmmm, distributer from Cortex said the company is suffering some loses and we will be greatly affected."

"Oh crap! Email me the details with his number. I am going to school now but don't be afraid to call." Chrystal said before leaving.

Around 11:37am, Laci walked in. Latoya looked at her.

"Hi, good morning, I am here to see Dwayne?" Laci smiled.

"I don't think that is possible. I was instructed not to disturb him. May I take a message?"

"Is he in a meeting or something?"

"I don't need to tell you that."

"Can you call him please? If you won't, I will. He wanted to see me."

"Who may I say?"

"Laci."

"Hello sir, I am sorry for disturbing you but there is one Laci here to see you. Okay sir. Follow me."

Laci followed Latoya who was frowning to Dwayne's office. Latoya knocked and opened the door. Laci entered.

"Hey bro in law." Laci smiled as she hugged Dwayne.

“Hey Laci, how are you?” Dwayne smiled.

“I am okay. Tired. Have to be putting in some late hours because I have hectic orders for flowers. How about you?”

“I am fairly okay. How is the family?”

“We are all okay. And how about your family?”

“They are okay.”

“How is your wife? I haven’t spoken to her lately. I hope marriage life is excellent!”

“That’s the problem. That’s one of the main reason I called you here.”

“What do you mean by that?”

“I didn’t want to involve you in this but Kaci is not the girl I fell in love with. She has changed. I haven’t had sex with my wife since the last day of our honeymoon. The nineteenth of December.”

“You are joking right?”

“No I am serious. All Kaci does is party and shop. I can’t touch her. I think I regretted getting married.”

"Why is Kaci doing this? I spoke to her."

"Do you know something?"

"Yes, Kaci was never in love with you. She only loved your money. I told her multiple of times to break it off with you because it didn't make any sense. I am sorry I should have said something but I thought she would have fallen in love with you by now."

"I think we rushed things."

"Even I said that. You guys were going too fast. Has Kaci ever told you she loved you?"

"No, but her actions proved she loved me."

"No Dwayne, Kaci herself said she didn't love you. I was not with that wedding. She even told me that I shouldn't come to her wedding. She is my twin but she is twisted. She loves you but only for your money."

"I cannot believe what I am hearing."

"I am so sorry. I blame myself. I should have said something to you."

"Don't say that. I wouldn't have believed you. I would have probably thought you were jealous based on what your sister told me about you."

"What did she tell you about me?"

"Can we talk over lunch?"

"Sure, my staff is okay for a few hours."

"How did you get here?"

"I took a bus."

"Okay can I drive you to a restaurant?"

"Sure."

"Let's go."

Laci left the office and Dwayne grabbed his jacket and kissed Kaci's picture on his desk before leaving the office. He went downstairs and caught Latoya starring down Laci.

"Latoya? What's that for?" Dwayne said startling her.

"Oh sir! Nothing!"

"I won't be in for some time. My sister in law and I are going out. If Kaci drops by give the file jacket I gave you yesterday."

"Okay sir."

"Laci, let's go."

Dwayne took Laci to a fine restaurant and they ate and talked. Around 1:09pm, Kaci walked into the office. She had on a very tight and short grey skirt, a royal blue chemise blouse and a pair of royal blue flat shoes with a royal blue hand bag and a file jacket in her hand.

"Latoya, I don't see Dwayne's car outside, do you have any idea where he went?"

"Good afternoon Mrs. Chisolm, he went out with his sister in law." Latoya said scornfully.

"Sister in law? Which sister in law?"

"I think she's your sister. Laci."

"She's back from Puerto Rico but decided to go out with my husband instead of calling me."

"Is everything okay?"

“Yes, may I have the keys to his office please?”

“Nicholas have them. Sir said I should give you this.”

“Thanks. Call Fiona and tell her to meet me in the office. Thanks.”

Kaci went to Nicholas’ office and collected the keys. She entered the office and sat on the desk as she spoke to Fiona. She spent two hours at the office. Just as she was about to leave the office, Dwayne entered. Kaci looked at him. He looked at her and went to the window.

“I scheduled a meeting with Amerax Group of Companies for Monday at 11:00am, the CEO Said he has been calling you but you weren’t answering. They were about to pull out of the deal. I also signed off the transfer for the products that were sent here two days ago.” Kaci said.

“Did you get the file I left with Latoya?” Dwayne asked without turning around.

“Yes. I’ll look into it when I get home. Enjoy the rest of your day.”

“Okay.”

Kaci stood looking at him.

“Dwayne?”

“Yes?”

“I am sorry about this morning. I know you are upset with me but I want to make it up to you?”

“I am working late tonight.”

“How late?”

“Very late. Don’t bother waiting up for me.”

“I can take dinner for you. We can work together and your work will be lighter.”

“No. That’s okay. You have your own work to do.”

“Okay.” Kaci said closing the door.

“Miss Robinson, your sister is here to see you.” Gabby said over the phone.

“Send her to the back. I am were the orchids are.” Laci said cheerfully.

“Do you know where the orchids are?”

“Yea I remember. Thanks.”

“Kaci! I am so excited to see you!” Laci said hugging her.

“When did you get back?” Kaci asked not hugging her back.

"Day before yesterday."

"I thought you weren't coming back."

"I have my establishment to get back to. Sis I haven't seen you in months. Mom misses you."

"You all know where I live?"

"You are never home Kaci. No one knows where you are these days."

"Oh so you are taking that as an invitation to fuck my husband?"

"Kaci! What are you talking about?"

"Don't try to hide it. I know everything! Spending over two hours with my husband today while I waited on him."

"Kaci I am not having an affair with your husband. I am in a relationship and I am happy. I don't want your husband. He was just asking for advice on how to make his wife love him."

"You are in a relationship? How contrary."

"Yes I have been dating for the past three months and I am happy."

"Who is that lucky guy? Because no one is ever lucky enough to have you?"

“The guy you rejected in Puerto Rico because he sold oranges.”

“You are so creepy. Can oranges maintain a family?”

“Kaci, we both own a club and a bakery in Puerto Rico. He no longer sells oranges. We are partners and the business is going well. He really loved you Kaci.”

“I have to go.”

“Feeling bad? Don’t worry! Dwayne won’t ever cheat on you! I just told him to give you space and hope you will come back to reality before it gets too late.”

“I should have never came here.”

“I’ll tell mom and dad you said hi!”

Laci smiled as she clipped some orchids.

That night Kaci sat waiting on Dwayne in a lingerie and her robe. Dwayne entered at 8:17pm. Kaci sat looking at him. The door knocked. Dwayne opened it.

“Dwayne hurry! I have VIP tickets to the most amazing party! I am waiting on you!” Chrystal said as she entered the room in a short black dress and a pair of red platform heels and a red party purse.

"I am going to have a quick shower!" Dwayne said running towards the bathroom.

"I'll find something for you to wear!"

"Knock yourself out!"

"What to choose? Oh hi Kaci, didn't know you were home."

"Where are you guys going?"

"To a party. Dwayne needs to go out being that you both are always fighting and you are always out."

"Cool. When I want to spend time with my husband, you are taking him away. That's great."

"Excuse me?"

"Nothing."

Kaci stepped out of the robe as Chrystal looked at her. Kaci got in a red flair dress and a pair of red flat shoes and got on her accessories. She took up her phone.

"Grace, change of plans. I am coming. No. Dwayne has a late meeting tonight so why not just stick to our plan. Yeah, I'll meet you girls there." Kaci said softly as she left the room.

"Kaci!"

She didn't look back. Chrystal felt away. Dwayne came from the bathroom.

"What did you find?" Dwayne asked.

"Just find something. I'll wait on you downstairs." Chrystal said.

"Why? What happened? Where is Kaci?"

"Nothing. She left."

<u>*CHAPTER 20*</u>

Sometime in May, Dwayne was in office. He was much stressed with work and his marriage. He had signed up for counselling but Kaci turned up at none of the sessions and so he gave up. He went on the phone. A few moments later the door knocked and opened.

"Yes sir?" Latoya said entering the office.

"Close the door behind you." Dwayne said.

"Okay. What's the problem sir?" Latoya asked as she slowly went towards the desk and sat.

Dwayne walked towards her and touched her leg. She had on a short black skirt with an aqua blouse. The top button was already open. Dwayne peeked on her breasts. Latoya began to button the top but Dwayne stopped her.

"Sir what are you doing?"

"I miss you."

"Sir, you are married. When I wanted you, you didn't want me and you went ahead and got married. My fiancé is back home now. I am done cheating on him. We are getting married soon sir."

"Why the fuck did I get married? Silly me."

"I can't do this sir. Even if you didn't get married I would have to stop because I am changing my life. I have to set a good example for my daughter. I am in love with her father."

"Relax! It's just like old times. Me, you and the office."

"Sir, you have a wife. I am getting married three months from now. Sir please stop!" Latoya shouted as Dwayne kissed her neck and Latoya slapped him.

"Lighten up!"

"What if your wife comes in and catches us in this manner?"
"I don't care! She doesn't love me anyways."

"Sir, your wife and my fiancé are business partners and she knows that. I cannot risk that."

"Sssssshhhh... Don't you miss me?"

“Yes I do but I...”

“That’s all I wanted to hear… I see it in your eyes.” Dwayne said as he opened her blouse and began to suck her breasts.

They made love in the office that afternoon for about two hours. When Dwayne got home he was smiling and had a glisten in his eyes. He skanked into the house around 6:30pm.

“Margret! I need a bottle of wine!” Dwayne shouted.

“Someone’s in a cheerful mood this evening! Red wine?” Margret smiled.

“No! White wine! OH YEAH!”

“Coming right up!”

“I’M THE MAN! WHOOOOIII!!!”

Chrystal was at school. Dwight was out of the country. Mrs. Chisolm was at a business party. Kaci came downstairs in a yellow shorts and a pink merino. She looked puzzled.

“Babe, what’s wrong with you?” Kaci asked.”

"Can't a man be happy for the first time in so many months?" Dwayne laughed as he turned the bottle to his head.

"Did you seal a deal?"

"What does it matter to you? I am in a good mood and I don't want you to spoil it! I just want to celebrate!"

"Well since you are in a good mood, can we go to one of my friend's birthday party and we can top it off with something special tonight?"

"Me? Oh no! I am going out with you tonight and pretend that everything is okay between us when it's not!"

"Please? I am sorry!"

"No Kaci. No. I am not going! Go by yourself!"

"Remember that we had promised Tammy that we'd be at her party?"

"Well Dwayne isn't in the mood to party with any of you!"

Kaci took her phone from her pocket. Margret and Pablo looked on.

"Hey, Tammy! I am so sorry girl but I won't be able to make it. I promise I'll make it up to you tomorrow. No. Dwayne is not feeling well, so I am staying with him. I know… a wife has to do what a wife has to do. I love you but I love my husband more.”

“Really? A wife has to do what a wife has to do? What type of wife are you? Certainly not the good wife.” Dwayne mocked.

“Babes, I know I haven’t been the best wife to you and I am really sorry about that. When I just met you I just wanted your money because I heard about your pattern with women and I decided not to love you. I just wanted to give you a taste of your own medicine but you fell in love with me. Dwayne I am sorry. I have decided to go counselling. I love you Dwayne. I really do. I want this marriage to work.”

“Excuse me!”

“Dwayne! I am talking to you!”

Kaci trailed Dwayne upstairs to their bedroom and an argument developed. The following morning Dwayne ran downstairs. Mrs. Chisolm and Chrystal were surprised to see him looking so ecstatic.

“Got the good stuff last night?” Mrs. Chisolm smiled.

“I am the man!” Dwayne laughed.

"Kaci what's wrong with you?" Chrystal asked as everyone looked at her including Dwayne.

"Nothing. Margret bring me two apples please?" Kaci said softly as she held her bag in her hand and keys in the other.

"Kaci, no breakfast this morning?" Mrs. Chisolm asked.

"No. I am not hungry. Thanks Margret. I have a long day today." Kaci sighed.

Dwayne looked at her in a concerned way.

"Kaci?" Mrs. Chisolm called as she walked towards the door.

"Leave her mom. Maybe bro gave her some good loving last night." Chrystal laughed as Dwayne took up his keys and walked from the house.

Dwayne wasn't going to work, he had on a sweatpants. He went to meet Laci at her work place. Kaci went to her office and spent the entire day there. She didn't go home until around 7:30pm. Dwayne was in bed texting but she only had a shower and went to bed.

"Kaci?" Dwayne called.

"What?" Kaci sniffed with her back turned.

"Are you okay?"

"Yes. Just had a long day."

"Are you sure?"

"Yes."

"Do you want to talk about it?"

"No."

"Okay."

"Yeah."

CHAPTER 21

The affair between Dwayne and Latoya went on for weeks. Either at the office or at a guest house. Kaci knew Dwayne was having an affair but she thought it was with Laci. She was trying to make her marriage work but it was too late. One Friday afternoon she sat inside Smoothies Paradise Yogurt on Barton Creek Square Village, in Austin Square to have yogurt.

"Hey, what's up?" Kaci said over the phone.

"Hi, Kaci, I am okay and you?" Laci responded.

"Nothing really. Hey listen, how busy are you?"

"Why?"

"I want to meet you. I am at Smoothies Paradise Yogurt a few blocks from your store."

"I'll be there in five minutes. I cannot be too busy for my sister."

"Okay, hurry. I'll treat you."

"Okay."

Kaci sat at a table playing a game on her tablet when her sister walked in and sat in front of her.

"Hi." Laci smiled as she sat.

"Hi, what do you want to eat?" Kaci said without smiling.

"Uhhh, I'll take uhhh, I'll have a raspberry muffin and a strawberry milkshake. But wait, it will trigger my sickness."

"Just take it. You have your medications don't you?"

"You are right. I have to take risks sometimes."

"Yea we all take some sort of risks every day and don't mind the consequences."

"What do you mean by that?"

"Nothing. Here is your order."

"Aren't you having anything?"

"I already ate something. I want to ask you something."

"Okay, go ahead."

"What kind of relationship do you have with Dwayne?"

"I don't have any relationship with him other than he is my brother in law and my friend."

"Are you sleeping with my husband?"

"No! Why would you ask me that?"

"Because I know my husband is cheating and he has been spending a lot of time with you. So it leaves me with no other options than to think it's with you."

"Kaci, I love your husband as a brother. I always have and I always will. I am not sleeping with your husband. For your information, I am moving to Puerto Rico by the end of the week. I am leaving mom in charge of my business. I am going to live with grandma and grandpa so I can see Pedro more often and oversee our business a lot more."

"What a cover! I don't believe you! You don't believe in living with a man before marriage and you aren't even engaged."

"I didn't say I was going to live with him, I said I am going to live with my grandparents. If you would spend time with your husband he wouldn't find the time to fuck his receptionist!"

"Now you are blaming her! Latoya is engaged. She is getting married three months from now. She is head over heels about Chris."

"You know her fiancé?"

"Yes I do. I actually work with him at the Golf Club! He's an investor and they come to the gym together every evening and she sometimes come to watch him play golf. So I just want you to leave my husband alone."

"I don't want your husband. He is not my type."

"I don't know why you don't just die! I wish you would succumb to your heart failure!"

"You don't mean that?"

"Yes I do! I hate you Laci! You have turned my husband's mind against me."

"Excuse me!" Laci left the table crying and blowing short.

"Laci!"

Kaci laughed and paid the bill. She went home. Laci went back to work and began to replant some flowers while thinking about what her sister had said to her.

"Laci? Are you okay?" Judean asked.

“Yes I am okay.” Laci responded blowing short.

“Laci, you are sweating and you are blowing short.”

“I am okay. I am just tired.”

“Do you want me to get your asthma pump?”

“Yes it’s in my bag.”

“Laci!” Tamara shouted as she caught her before she fell.

“Call the ambulance!” Melonie shouted to Judean.

Laci was unconscious and blood was flowing from her nostrils.

CHAPTER 22

Kaci was at home reading a fashion magazine in the sitting room, when Chrystal ran frantically into the house.

"CC, what's wrong?" Margret asked.

"Where is Kaci?" Chrystal asked.

"I just served her juice in the sitting room. Is everything okay?"

"Her sister is in the hospital. No one can get her phone."

"Oh my God!"

"Kaci! Kaci!"

"Yes! What do you want now?"

"Your parents have been trying to get your phone for the past twenty minutes. Where is your phone?"

"It's upstairs. What do they want?"

"Your sister is admitted in the hospital."

“Okay.”

“Your sister, I mean your twin sister is admitted in the hospital and all you have to say is okay?”

“I have bigger problems to deal with.”

“Mom is also at the hospital!”

“So?”

“You know it’s pointless talking to you! I am going to the hospital!”

“Good!”

At the hospital.

“Mona, please calm down! This is not good for you.” Mrs. Chisolm tried consoling.

“Why didn’t she tell me she has asthma and pneumonia? I could have dealt with it Marsha but not like this.” Mona cried.

“Don’t worry. She will be okay. You have to be strong.”

Chrystal walked in and hugged Damion. Patrick was pacing the hospital floor. He wasn’t speaking.

"Chrystal, where is Kaci? I thought I sent you to get her." Mrs. Chisolm asked.

"Mom, I did. I tried. I am sorry to say this Mrs. Robinson, but your daughter doesn't care. She said she has bigger problems to deal with." Chrystal sighed.

"No! That is not Kaci! Kaci-Ann loves Laci-Ana! You are mixing her up!"

"I am sorry."

Chrystal walked off and Mrs. Chisolm hugged Mona. Just then Dwayne came inside the hospital. He searched the room with his eyes. He saw Tawney, Shelly, Grace, Mona, Patrick, his mother, his sister and Damion but he didn't see Kaci.

"CC, where is Kaci?" Dwayne asked grabbing Chrystal by her arm.

"Ouch! She's at home." Chrystal said annoyingly.

"What do you mean at home? Why isn't she here?"

"She doesn't want to. She said she has bigger problems to deal with. Excuse I am getting a call. Hello? No, no, I am at the hospital. Yes I have it. Okay let me go to my car and I'll call you and give you the info. Okay no problem." Chrystal said as she went outside.

The doctor came out of the room.

"Mr. and Mrs. Robinson,-everyone encircled him- the patient is critical but we are hoping that she will respond to the treatments. We have some more tests to run on her to find out any other complications but for now we are just hoping for the best." The doctor stated.

"Can I see her now?" Mona asked.

"Yes you all can see her, but be mindful she won't respond to you now." The doctor said before walking away.

Mona, Patrick, Tawney and Shelly went into the room. Laci's eyes were closed. Everyone left except for Mona and Patrick.

"KACI! KACI!" Dwayne shouted as he entered the house followed by his mother and sister.

Margret and Pablo pointed to the direction she was in. She was still in the living room in the dark.

"Lalalalalalala, Lalalalalalala." They heard Kaci singing in the living room.

Dwayne entered turning on the lights which revealed she was sitting in a rocking chair.

"You are sick!" Dwayne shouted.

"Talking to me?" Kaci smiled.

"You are a wicked, ungrateful, disgusting bitch!"

"What did I do?"

"Can you imagine your sister is admitted in the hospital and you didn't even bother to show up? She is your twin sister! What have you turned into?"

"Everyone has this time span on earth maybe God is ready for her now."

"Do you she is battling for life right now?"

"Yes I do. She always has been. I know she has asthma and pneumonia. I have known for years. I didn't tell her to eat that muffin and drink that strawberry milkshake today. She knows that strawberry is a trigger for her asthma."

"You know all of this and you didn't tell anyone?"

"Ooooops, but it wasn't my place to do so. I told her to get married to a rich guy but she didn't listen. He could have paid for her treatment. Her rheumatic heart disease would have been under control right now. Oh well."

"Your sister has RHD, asthma and pneumonia and you told no one."

"She is fragile. God is probably just ready for her."

SLAP!!!!!!

"Ouch! What's that for?" Kaci screamed.

"That's for your sister! CC, call the hospital! I am going to transfer some money there. She has to go into surgery right away. Tell them I am sending a surgeon there to complete the heart surgery. Dwayne inform her parents." Mrs. Chisolm said walking off.

"You sick my stomach!" Dwayne said.

"I am more convinced that you are fucking her! I just wish she would die so I can have my husband back!" Kaci shouted storming upstairs.

"Kaci!" Dwayne called running towards the stairs when Chrystal grabbed his hand.

"Are you cheating on Kaci, with her sister? I can't believe you. That is why the poor girl doesn't care! That's disgusting Dwayne!"

"CC, I am not!"

"Do you know I believe her?"

"Why?"

"Because that's in your nature. When you told me you are getting married I was shocked because you are a womanizer. I don't know how you are going to get out of this mess."

"CC, let me go!"

Dwayne ran upstairs as Chrystal looked on. He entered the room and saw Kaci throwing some vases on the ground. He saw roses on the bed and candles on the floor. There was a bottle of champagne on a table with strawberries, chocolate and whipped cream. There was a lingerie on the bed. Kaci was crying and breaking some glasses. Dwayne walked towards her and held her.

"Let me go!" Kaci screamed.

"Kaci calm down. Look at me!" Dwayne said.

"No!"

"Kaci I want to love you again. I always wanted you but you always pushed me away."

"Because you are fucking my sister! Ever since she came back from Puerto Rico! You don't love me! Just leave me alone!"

"This was romantic of you but I am sorry it turned out this way."

"Dwayne just…"

Dwayne started to kiss her. They made love that night.

"Good morning baby." Dwayne said rolling over to kiss Kaci.

"Good morning hon." Kaci smiled kissing him as she laid on his chest.

"How was your night?"

"It was the best I had in months I guess?'

"You guess?"

"Yes… Dwayne can I ask you a question?"

"Sure."

"I want you to be honest, are you cheating on me?"

"No."

"Are you sure?"

"I am not cheating on you. I am losing love for you but I am not cheating."

"Okay. I am going to work on our marriage. I want back that love that you had for me."

"You will have to work hard."

"I promise that I am going to."

"I have to see you do that first being that it is coming from you."

"Whatever."

Kaci got out of bed and stepped on a piece of glass.

"Ouch!" Kaci screamed.

"Kaci!" Dwayne said as he pulled the glass from her foot.

They got dressed and left for work.

"Margret can you clean my room please. Be careful, there are splinters on the floor." Dwayne said as he went towards the door.

"Dwayne what happened in that room last night?" Mrs. Chisolm asked.

"Kaci broke some glasses."

Chrystal looked at him and he walked away.

CHAPTER 23

Everything seemed to be going well between Kaci and Dwayne. Kaci still hadn't gone to see her sister, who was still in the hospital. Dwayne was still cheating and he would come home late every evening. They went counselling but Dwayne would be absent for most of the sessions. Mrs. Chisolm hardly spoke to Kaci.

"Kaci, I understand what you are going through." Chrystal said hugging her one morning.

"What are you talking about?" Kaci asked.

"Living with a cheating husband. It must be hard."

"It's okay. I am- I-I everything is okay."

"I know it's not but don't worry, I am here for you."

"Dwayne is not cheating."

"Well your sister is still in the hospital so maybe he isn't now."

"You knew about them?"

"I heard when you said it to him the night she got admitted."

"Excuse me!" Kaci said covering her mouth and running upstairs.

Chrystal looked at her. When Kaci came from the bathroom, she saw Dwayne's phone on the bed. It was lit and she saw a message. She took up the phone. She saw some messages from Latoya with some hearts. The message that caught her eyes read: '*That dick was so good yesterday that I couldn't stop thinking about you. I can't wait for you to divorce your wife so that I can break off my engagement and be with you my love. I love you*' Dwayne's response was: '*I love you too. The divorce will take time but it will come through. You'll soon have a place in the mansion.*' Kaci's eyes filled with water. She threw the phone on the bed. She took up a notepad and began writing as tears flowed from her eyes, afterwards she grabbed her phone and purse and ran downstairs. Dwayne looked at her.

"I am going to the office now. I'll drop by sometime today." Dwayne said on the landline going upstairs for his phone.

"Kaci, are you okay?" Chrystal asked.

"Yes!" Kaci cried going towards the door.

"Kaci, you don't want the meal I prepared?" Margret asked.

"No! I just feel for grapes."

"But that's all you have been eating!"

"Is it just me or is Kaci pregnant?" Chrystal asked Margret.

"I don't know Ma'am."

"I intend to find out. I'll search their room when Dwayne leaves."

"Are you sure you want to do that?"

"I am positive."

"Okay."

"Yes and you are going to help me."

"CC, no!"

"You know I don't take no's from you. Bye Dwayne. Have a nice day at work."

"Bye CC." Dwayne said texting on his phone.

Kaci stopped at Lakeway City Park. She walked into the park crying and sat under a tree near the lake. She was texting Grace. Grace called her.

"Yeah?" Kaci answered.

"Where the fuck are you?" Grace shouted.

"Why do you care?"

"Kaci, don't you fucking play with me! I said where the fuck are you?"

"It doesn't matter."

"Oh never mind. I just saw your fucking car. Because you are one crazy bitch! Don't you move, I am coming!"

"Whatever!"

Kaci threw the phone in the water.

"Why did you do that?" Sabrina shouted.

"Sabrina what are you doing here?" Kaci asked.

"I was with Grace. We were coming to look for you and to hear you saying you are going to take your life. Kaci what is going on?"

"Nothing."

"KACI!" Grace shouted as she slid beside Kaci. "What is going on?" she added.

"Guys just leave me alone!" Kaci cried as Grace hugged her.

"Kaci, talk to us. What is wrong?"

"I am cruel person. I knew my sister was sick and I did nothing to help her. I told her that as soon as I got married I would pay for a surgery and I let material things get in my way. I don't even have the guts to face her. She has been in the hospital for over two months and I can't find the courage to visit her. My brother cursed me. My dad cursed me. My aunt cursed me and my mom doesn't want to talk to me. I am the cause why my sister is in the hospital."

"Kaci stop blaming yourself. Laci is sick and that's why she is in the hospital." Sabrina sighed.

"No! She didn't have to be there. I allowed her to drink strawberry milkshake. She is supposed to avoid it and I told her to take the risk and I told her I wanted her to die because I thought she was having an affair with my husband. That night when I heard she was in the hospital I couldn't visit her because I couldn't believe that my wish came through. I didn't mean it."

"Kaci, your wish didn't come through. Laci is still alive. Her surgery went well last week. She is just under observation because she is not talking to anyone. I visit on a daily basis." Grace said.

"It's all because of me. My mother in law hardly talks to me. My husband is cheating on me with his secretary and he is planning to divorce me for her. I am horrible wife. I cannot raise a baby by myself."

"You're pregnant?" Sabrina and Grace exclaimed.

"Yes I am ten weeks."

"Kaci, you cannot take your life. You have an innocent life bringing. Kaci please think about it. This baby will you bring you joy and peace even if you have to do it alone." Sabrina said.

"Kaci, we all knew that Dwayne was a player. Once a player always a player. You won't lose anything if he divorces you. You are legally bounded and maybe he doesn't know but half of his assets belong to you and now that you are pregnant you will have to get even more. See you don't love him and you are gaining what you went for. You will be succeeding at your game." Grace said

"No! I don't want to divorce him! I am in love with him!"

"Say what?" Grace exclaimed.

"Yes you heard me. I am in love with Dwayne but he is in love with his receptionist. It just better if I take my life."

"Kaci don't. We love you. Do one thing for me. Will you?" Grace asked.

"What's that?"

"Go and talk to your sister. Apologize to her and ask her forgiveness. Take your life after."

"Grace! You can't say that." Sabrina said.

"But if I talk to her I can't kill myself after. It will drive her crazy. Laci loves me."

"Kaci, if you don't meet her and then she gets the news that you committed suicide, don't you think she'll blame herself. Go and make peace with your twin sister. Where's your phone?"

"She threw it in the water." Sabrina said.

"Kaci. I am driving you to the hospital because you are in no condition to drive, I might just book you to seek medical attention." Grace said angrily.

"What about your car?"

"I am driving my car."

"So what about my car?"

"It can stay right here. No one will trouble it. Let's go."

"But…"

"No buts Kaci. Let's go!"

CHAPTER 24

"Margret let's go!" Chrystal said going up the stairs.

"I still don't think this is a good idea. You know how Dwayne stays and his wife is just like him! We don't even know where she went!" Margret said going up behind her.

"Oh please! We all know that whenever Kaci leaves this house, she doesn't return until night. Let's go!"

They entered the room and began to search.

Grace arrived at the hospital with Kaci. They sent her inside and waited in the parking lot. When she entered the hospital, she saw her mother, Tawney and Shelly.

"Hi mom?" Kaci cried.

"What are you doing here?" Tawney exclaimed as her mother turned her back.

"I am sorry guys. Mom just look at me. I know I am the worst daughter ever and the worst niece. I hate myself for it. I am sorry I didn't tell you earlier that Laci was sick but she didn't want you to know. What was I supposed to do, break my sister's trust? Mom, I know Dwayne told you everything but I was jealous of Laci. I am sorry I said I wanted her to die. I regretted every words I said to her. Mom, how would you feel if you committed a mistake and grandma hated you for life or you did something bad to Aunt Tawney and she despised you forever? It has taken a long time for me to realize what you all mean to me and that's why I am apologizing. Don't lose your faith in me ma. I am trying to pull myself out of the mess I have made but I can't move on with myself if you don't forgive me. Mom, the cycle of the perfect apology starts with a mistake followed by a regret followed by a sorry followed by forgiveness. I started the first three, please complete the last one mom. I am sorry." Kaci cried.

Tawney and Shelly were teary eyed. Mona walked towards her and slapped her across her face.

"Do all you want mom but just forgive me please?"

"I forgive you." Mona cried as she hugged Kaci tightly.

Kaci hugged her back.

"Mom I am really, really sorry."

"Stop the crying. Your speech really touched me. I am happy you found your mistake."

"Thanks mom. Aunt?"

"Come here. Who am I not to forgive my little princess? You are my princess and Laci is my cowgirl." Tawney said hugging her.

Kaci ran and threw up in a flower pot.

"Kaci are you okay?" Mona asked.

"Yes I am fine." Kaci replied as she threw up again.

"Are you pregnant?"

"No. It's probably something I ate. Can I see Laci please?"

"Yes you can, but she isn't talking."

"Okay."

Kaci entered the room. Everyone stood at the door watching. She sat on the bed. She held her hand.

"Laci, I know I am the worst sister ever and I know you are hearing me and I have something to say to you. I love you. I knew the last time we spoke I said I hated you but the truth I am crazy over you. Being your twin sister is the greatest thing I'll ever achieve in my life. Every single moment with you is to be treasured. The bond that we have with each other is one that nobody can measure. You held my hand when I was scared, you got me ready when I wasn't even prepared. I remember when you carried me when we were walking and the journey was so long. You always fought for me even when I was wrong. You really amaze me even though I don't tell you Laci, with your tender heart and your loving way. I regretted the way I treated you, you deserve so much more, and I really hope you will forgive me. There is so much more that I can say if only I could find the sentence. Right now all I can do is offer you my repentance. You are my rock, my everything, with you I am safe and sound, you are the girl I can always lean on, the force that keeps me on the ground. You have been here all my life and I know we will never part, please promise me you won't leave me. I guess I just told you this to let you know I love you with all my heart and I am sorry." Kaci cried.

Kaci still held Laci's hand. To everyone's surprise, Laci held back Kaci's hand.

"Kaci, I have forgiven you. I love you." Laci tried smiling.

"You responded." Kaci smiled wiping her tears.

"Kaci can I ask you something?"

"No. I know what you are going to ask. Yes I do love Dwayne but that relationship doesn't matter to me. I am just happy I have my sister."

"Go and save your marriage if you love him."

"But I have to be with you."

"Go and save your marriage. I think Dwayne needs you more than I do right now. Go!"

Kaci ran from the room. Everyone was shocked as they were clueless. They entered the room where Laci was. Kaci went to the car park.

"Take me to Dwayne's office now!" Kaci ordered.

"Laci sent you right?" Grace asked.

"Yes."

"I always loved that girl!" Sabrina laughed.

"Chrystal I found something!" Margret said holding a paper.

"Give it to me! Let's read what's here."

Chrystal sat on the bed and Margret sat on the chair. Chrystal began reading:

'Chisolm Mansion, Lakeway Terrace, 765487, Austin, Texas, U.S.A.

July 21, 2017. 10:01am.

Dear Dwayne Chisolm,

Most of the times I wish I was dead. I hate myself so fucking much every day. My thoughts are killing me. I feel lost inside myself. I don't want to be here anymore. I am tired of this. I think too much. I am never okay these days. Lately I have just been forcing a smile. I always cared but I always got hurt and that's why I hid my true feelings from you because I knew your nature and I didn't want you to hurt me, but instead I am hurting myself because I fell in love with you when you fell out of love with me.

You know people say that suicide is a permanent answer to a temporary problem, but what if that problem isn't temporary? Dwayne I grew to love you but I guess it was too late. I am sorry I accused you of sleeping with Laci. I caused her to be in the hospital so I want you tell her that I love her and I wish her all the best. Tell my mom that I am sorry and Uhmmm she'll have less pain since I'll be gone. Tell my father that I love him and my brother, tell him the same. Tawney my aunt, she is a blessing. Your mom hates my guts, just tell her I am sorry for being a bitch and your sister, Chrystal she can be a bitch but a good one though. She is wise because she is the only person who figured something was wrong with me but I couldn't share it with her. Your father isn't around much but he welcomed me into his home and I want you tell him I am sorry. Grace and Sabrina I may text them and tell them but if not inform them. They were my chicas for life.

Dwayne you lied to me. You told me you weren't cheating but I have proof. I hope Latoya will make you very happy because as the message on phone stated that she loved your dick and you responded confirming my divorce so I am making it easier for you. You will just be a widower. I was waiting for the right time to show you my ultrasound with our baby (it's in the drawer on my dressing table) but it won't be possible because you are never home these days. I am not a good wife nor daughter in law not even a good daughter or sister but just know that I loved you and this baby would have loved you too. I am ten weeks pregnant by the way. I wish you and Latoya a prosperous life.

By the time you are reading this, I'll be gone. I'll make it easier for you, I am planning on jumping into the lake by Lakeway City Park.

Your frustrated pregnant wife,

Kaci-Ann Ariana Robinson-Chisolm.

Love always.'

"Oh no! What are we going to do?" Margret asked.

"Dwayne isn't answering! I am going to the park." Chrystal cried frantically running downstairs.

"I'll call your mom!" Margret screamed.

"Yea whatever!" Chrystal said grabbing her keys and running outside.

"What happened?" Pablo asked.

"Kaci, has committed suicide! We found the letter under the pillow."

"Omg! What should we do?"

"I don't know. Sir Dwayne isn't answering. I am going to call Madame now. Chrystal went to look for her. She said in the letter at the park."

CHAPTER 25

Chrystal arrived at the park and saw Kaci's vehicle. Her purse was on the seat.

Chrystal panicked as she called Dwayne who still wasn't answering.

"Yes mom!" Chrystal answered.

"Where are you?" Mrs. Chisolm asked.

"At the park."

"I am coming. Have you seen her?"

"No mom, only her car and her purse is in it."

"I am on my way."

"Okay."

Grace pulled up in the parking lot of Dwayne's office. Kaci walked in. Latoya wasn't at her desk. The security was surprised to see her but he didn't say anything. Grace entered the building followed by Sabrina.

"Kaci!" Grace called as she began the stairs.

"What?" Kaci answered.

"Want me to come with you?"

"No! I don't think they would be doing this at the office knowing I drop by regularly."

"Okay baby girl. We'll be waiting right here."

"Okay mamacita!"

Kaci went upstairs and saw a few workers who looked at her shockingly. She smiled and passed them. Kaci stood at the door and overheard Dwayne on the phone.

"Yes Mr. Denzel, I need those divorce papers to sign. Yes you can drop them off today." Dwayne said.

"Dwayne I can't wait for us to be together permanently. I want to stop hiding." Latoya said.

"Soon baby. Soon. I love you." Dwayne said.

"Mrs. Chisolm, what are you doing here?" Nicholas asked.

"So you are aware of it too?" Kaci asked.

"It wasn't my place to talk."

"So when she is in here, who is at the front desk?"

"The security."

"Oh so he is getting a double salary?"

"I don't know."

Kaci pushed the key into the keyhole and turned the lock. The door opened. Dwayne was shirtless and Latoya was blouse less. They were in a compromising position. They were kissing and fondling each other. They were on the desk. Chrystal arrived downstairs and saw Grace and Sabrina. She was crying.

"CC, what's wrong with you?" Grace asked.

"I don't know how to break this." Chrystal cried.

"Is it something with your mom?"

"No, it's Kaci. I think she committed suicide. I found the letter."

"Calm down. We stopped her. She is upstairs."

"Really?"

"We stopped her in time, just as she threw away her phone in the lake."

"I am going up. Let me call mom."

Chrystal ran up the stairs. She saw Kaci just as her mother answered. She didn't know what was going on inside the office.

"Yes mom! I saw her. I'll explain everything to you. We are at the office." Chrystal said entering the office.

Kaci looked at her and so did Dwayne and Latoya. Kaci was videoing them.

"Kaci! CC!" Dwayne shouted jumping off the table, pulling up his zipper and grabbing his shirt.

Latoya grabbed her blouse and began to get dressed after she pulled her skirt down.

"Dwayne! I did not expect this!" Chrystal exclaimed.

"I can explain!" Dwayne said.

"What are you going to explain? Take a look at this! Your wife was about to commit suicide! Thank God for Grace and Sabrina who saved her!" Chrystal shouted as she pushed the letter at him.

Kaci was shocked to see the letter as she had no idea that Chrystal was in her bedroom. She was silent. Tears ran from her eyes as Dwayne read the letter. Latoya tried to leave the office but Chrystal barred her. Employees were gathered at the door.

"Kaci, I didn't know you were pregnant." Dwayne said trying to touch her as Latoya looked on.

"Don't touch me!" Kaci said stepping backwards.

"Kaci, I am sorry. I didn't know you felt all this way about me. Please forgive me."

"No! You lied to me! I asked you if you were cheating and you said no! Excuse me!" Kaci said pushing her way out of the office.

She ran downstairs.

"Grace take me somewhere. Take me anywhere!" Kaci screamed.

"What?" Grace asked.

"I think she just saw them cheating. Let's go!" Sabrina said

The three girls walked through the door.

"Dwayne, why did you?" Chrystal asked.

"I said I am sorry. Now let me go stop my wife." Dwayne stated.

"No! Let her go. You are going to divorce her anyways."

"She is bringing my baby. I can't divorce her."

"Dwayne what about me?" Latoya asked.

"Oh just shut up! Don't you see what is happening here! I love my wife!" Dwayne shouted.

"Nicholas! Get in here now!" Chrystal ordered.

"Yes miss." Nicholas said entering quickly.

"Document ten, get it printed and place it in an envelope. Pronto!"

Nicholas left.

"Now why are you here? Don't you all have work to do?" Chrystal shouted at the employees as she slammed the door.

“So how long have you been fucking my brother?”

“Is this really necessary?” Latoya asked.

“Just answer my question.”

“CC, that is not necessary.” Dwayne said.

“You shut up! Mom will deal with you! Latoya I am talking to you! How would your fiancé feel to find out you were sleeping with his business partner’s husband?”

“Excuse me?” Nicholas said interrupting them.

“Thank you Nick. Go through her file and get the required cheque. Take it to me and I’ll sign it.”

“Okay.”

“Latoya this is yours. Your service is no longer required here. I want you to go downstairs and clear your desk. If you have anything in the breakroom clear it also. I am going to need your employee badge and ID.”

“What? You can’t fire me! You didn’t hire me!”

"Somebody hasn't read their contract. When my father hired you, the contract stated that, my father, my mother, Dwayne or I can fire you and recently an addition was made by Dwayne himself, Kaci can fire you. Now get packing. Dwayne go home and have a shower. I need to get this office sanitized."

Latoya left the office crying. Dwayne had an argument with Chrystal. Dwayne went downstairs.

"Dwayne, please talk to your sister." Latoya cried.

"I can't! It's over between us."

"Dwayne you can't do this to me! The divorce is already in process."

"I just canceled it. I am sorry Latoya but I love my wife and she is bringing my baby."

"Dwayne you can't do this to me."

"Good bye Latoya."

Dwayne walked from the office.

CHAPTER 26

Latoya handed her badges and ID to Chrystal with tears in her eyes.

"Nicholas, print some memos and inform all staff members to attend a mandatory staff meeting Monday at 8:30am sharp and I need a list of all the employees because if anyone is absent I'll be taking drastic measures. I have to get dad here, he needs to be at this meeting." Chrystal said before whispering to herself.

"Okay Miss Chisolm. I'll get that done right away." Nicholas said running upstairs.

"Kaci, we cannot allow you to do that." Sabrina said.

"You are pregnant Kaci, drinking is not going to solve your problem." Grace said.

"How would you feel if you walked into your husband's office and saw him on top of his receptionist? No one knows what I am feeling inside." Kaci cried.

"Kaci, I am going to be honest. This is all your fault. You were the one who pushed Dwayne away. I know that Dwayne tried his best. He has simply given up on you, but he is sorry because deep down Dwayne still loves you." Grace said.

"How do you know that?"

"Dwayne has been meeting with me lately. I didn't know he was cheating though else I would have said something to you and I would have talked to him about it. But Dwayne loves you but this was all your fault. You went into this marriage with one aim." Grace said.

"I am such a horrible person." Kaci cried as she placed her head on Sabrina's shoulder.

"No you are not. Now I am going to take you to the beach and you are going to forget all about this."

"I don't want to go to any beach."

"I am not asking you; I am telling you." Grace said as she closed the door and went towards the front.

"Pablo!" Mrs. Chisolm called.

"Yes Madame?" Pablo answered.

"Come with me. I am going drop you at Lakeway City Park and I want you to take Kaci's car home. I have a spare key. I have to go to the store."

"Okay Madame."

They left. Dwayne was at a bar drinking as he tried calling Kaci's phone.

"Dude, you need to go home! Drinking is not going to help you!" Chad said.

"She was about to commit suicide because of me. Why didn't I see this coming? Now she is not taking my calls!" Dwayne shouted.

"And whose fault is that? D, look no one told you to cheat especially with that bitch! What do you see in her by the way?"

"Chad you don't understand do you?"

"Dwayne, I am a man and if I am going to cheat on Ashley I would not choose my receptionist. Those girls are too easy. You have been married for like seven months since yesterday and you have been cheating since three months now. I spoke to dwag. I did."

"Where the fuck is Kaci?!" Dwayne shouted throwing the glass into the wall as everyone looked at him.

"Hey, calm down! Kaci is probably with her friends. She's upset! Do you think she'd take any calls from you after she caught you butt naked on your receptionist?"

“I wasn’t butt naked.”

“Whatever man! I spoke to you! Who the fuck cheats in their office when their wife has keys to that office?”

“Hey what’s going on here?” Chris interrupted.

“Kaci finally caught him cheating and Chrystal found this in their room.” Chad said.

“No! Where is Kaci? She didn’t…”

“No, Grace stopped her but she caught him after. No one knows where she is now. She isn’t taking any calls.”

“No! Dwayne how could you? Kaci is pregnant!” Chris said as Dwayne and Chad looked at him.

“Tell me you just read that?” Dwayne asked.

“No, Kaci told me the day she found out. She was scared to tell you, you weren’t even at home with her. I don’t need to read that to know. If you had spent more time with your wife than with that bitch you would have known.”

“But dude the girl was pushing him away.” Chad said.

“I spoke to Kaci and Kaci had started to get attach before Dwayne started cheating. But I thought everything was okay now.”

“I didn’t know friends kept secret now!” Dwayne shouted as he jumped from the stool and walked through the door.

“Dwayne!” Chad and Chris called out; he ignored them and left.

“What was that for?” Chad asked.

“It’s the truth. If you don’t like it’s your luck!” Chris said leaving the bar.

“Dad, you are needed home ASAP!” Chrystal cried.

“What’s wrong?” Dwight asked.

“Everything daddy.”

“Okay baby girl, listen I was actually on my way home. I wanted to surprise you guys. Don’t say anything to anyone. I am like an hour away. I am driving so I am going to hang up now.”

“Okay daddy. I love you.”

“I love you too baby girl.”

At the hospital, Mona, Damion and Shelly were in the room with Laci when the door opened.

"Hello everyone." Pedro smiled entering the room with a bouquet of flowers.

"Hey Pedro. I didn't know you were coming." Mona said.

"I can't stay away too long."

"Babe, who is in charge of the business?" Laci asked.

"Don't worry about that. I have that all covered. What I need is for you to get better." Pedro said kissing Laci on her cheek.

"Thank you. The flowers are lovely."

"Not as lovely as you."

"Pedro. But seriously who is in charge of the business if you are here?"

"If you insist. Your grandma."

"My grandma?! You are joking right?"

"No I am not. Your grandmother is okay. In fact she sent me here. She told me not to listen to you and that she will take care of everything."

"Laci, I asked grandma to send him to you. You both are workaholics and you need time. It was my idea and grandma was totally with it." Shelly said.

"Excuse me, I am here to discharge Laci-Ana. She can go home now. She took a miraculously recovery this morning." The doctor said.

"That was because of Kaci." Laci whispered to herself.

"Thank you doctor." Mona said as the doctor left.

"No!" Laci screamed.

"What's wrong?" Everyone asked.

"Kaci is in trouble! I need to see Kaci!"
"Kaci is okay." Shelly said.

"No she is not! Kaci is hurting! I need my sister!"

"Laci, Kaci is okay."

"I need to call her. Give me my phone!"

Laci grabbed the phone from Mona and dialed Kaci's number.

"She is not answering. The phone is off."

“Maybe she is busy.” Shelly said.

“No! Kaci’s phone is never off. Something is wrong with her.”

“Let me call Dwayne.” Mona sighed.

“What?” Dwayne answered.

“Dwayne? What’s going on? Why did you answer me like that?”

“I am sorry. I thought it was someone else.”

“Dwayne, where is Kaci?”

“I don’t know.”

“What do you mean you don’t know? Where is my daughter?”

“I can’t find her okay! I don’t know where she went!”

“Listen to me and listen good, you better not be hurting my daughter!”

“Dwayne where is my sister?” Laci shouted as she grabbed the phone from Mona.

“Laci I don’t know. I messed up okay. And it was all her fault!”

“Hello? Dwayne? Hello? He hang up on me.”

"Let's do one thing. We take you home and then we call Marsha or Chrystal. We can call the residence number and see if she is home."

CHAPTER 27

Dwayne was at the park throwing stones in to the lake as he recalled moments with Kaci before they got married and when she walked in on him cheating. He was untidy. He was drunk. It was 8:10pm when he staggered inside.

"Sir let me help you." Pablo said holding his arm.

"Leave me alone!" Dwayne shouted, just as he received a slap across his cheek.

"What the fuck is that for?" Dwayne shouted.

"Is this how I grew you? I thought you were changed man but I was wrong? Where did I go wrong in raising my children? Chrystal doesn't mind embarrassing me when we go out and my son doesn't stop playing games with these girls! I know Kaci was wrong but cheating? Why didn't you divorce her? Why the office? Why the receptionist? Isn't she engaged?" Mrs. Chisolm cried as Chrystal looked on.

"Honey calm down. Remember you have hypertension." Mr. Chisolm said hugging her.

"Dad? You are here?" Dwayne smiled.

"Don't you smile with me. I can't believe you did this! I didn't expect this from you son! Where is Kaci?"

"I DON'T KNOW! ISN'T SHE HOME!"

"No! She is not! Kaci almost committed suicide because of you! Laci and Mona are worried for her and I cannot tell them where she is because I don't know. Now this explains you coming in late and when Chrystal asks to come and help you, you turn her down! Dwayne I have lost all trust in you! I have lost all the respect that I had for you! Lord wherever Kaci is please guide and protect her with my grandchild." Mrs. Chisolm shouted as she slapped Dwayne across his cheek once again.

Dwayne went back through the door slamming it.

"Dwayne!" Mrs. Chisolm shouted.

"Dwayne!" Chrystal shouted as she ran behind him. "Dwayne where are you going?" she continued.

"Anywhere but here." Dwayne shouted.

"You are not driving anywhere!" Chrystal said pulling the keys from his hand.

"CC! Give me ma keys!"

“No!”

“I’ll walk then!”

“You won’t go far!”

Dwayne went inside and stormed upstairs to his bedroom. He slammed the door. He tried calling Kaci’s phone once again.

“Kaci I am going to the bathroom. I’ll be back. Sabrina is right over there on the phone, okay? Please eat something.” Grace said as she left the table.

“Waiter!” Kaci called.

“Yes ma’am?” the answered.

“Three shots of your strongest liquor in this drink! Quickly!”

“Okay, I’ll be back.”

The waiter returned and Kaci tipped him. She drank the drink from the glass and took two Tylenol that she took from Grace’s bag. After ten minutes Grace returned.

“Kaci? Kaci?” Grace called.

“What’s wrong with her?” Sabrina asked.

"I don't know. She looks like she is drunk. Waiter, did she drink something?" Grace asked.

"Yes, she just ordered three shots of our strongest drink." The waiter said.

"Omg! We have to get her home. Thank you. Here is your money. Keep the change." Grace said.

"Leeeeeeaaaaaave meeeeee alone! I am fiiiiiiiiinnnnnneee…" Kaci said.

"Nope, we are going home." Sabrina said as she and Grace lifted her and walked towards the door.

"Noooooooooooo!"

"I am not arguing with you. My battery is dead! I can't call Dwayne and I don't know his number from my head." Grace said as she and Sabrina placed Kaci in the car.

"I don't have his number since I changed my phone yesterday." Sabrina said closing the door.

At 10:45pm the doorbell rang and Pablo opened it. Sabrina and Grace entered with Kaci. Dwayne and his parents were in the sitting room.

"Mom, I am sorry okay." Dwayne said.

"I know you are. I am just upset and worried. Maybe if I was speaking to her she would have confided in me." Mrs. Chisolm cried.

"Son, I just want you to be more responsible. I want you to think before you do anything. You are my CEO and you have to be responsible." Mr. Chisolm said.

"I know guys. And I am sorry. I am going to do my best to make my marriage work once Kaci comes back and I am going to be responsible as of tonight." Dwayne said as his mother hugged him.

"Let me go! I can walk!" Kaci said pouting.

"You couldn't a minute ago." Grace said.

Kaci staggered into the house.

"Madame, can I get you some coffee?" Pablo asked.

"No! I don't waaaaaaant anything! I am finnnnnne!" Kaci shouted.

"Kaci!" Chrystal shouted running towards her.

"Don't touch meeeeee!" Kaci shouted.

Dwayne and his parents ran from the sitting room.

"Kaci!" Dwayne said running to her.

"Stop! Leeeeeeaaaaaave meeeeee alone!" Kaci shouted as she started the stairs.

"What's wrong with her?" Mrs. Chisolm asked.

"She had three shots of a strong liquor, when I went to the bathroom." Grace said.

"Why did you have liquor around her?"

"Do you think I would have liquor around her? One I know she is pregnant. And secondly I don't allow Kaci to drink more than a Smirnoff Ice, her head is very light."

Kaci was sitting on the stairs and Mr. Chisolm sat beside her. He spoke to her and she soon broke down in tears. He hugged her. Mrs. Chisolm called her mother and informed her. Chrystal took some tea Kaci and Mr. Chisolm fed it to her. Dwayne stood looking at her before he went upstairs to his bedroom. Grace and Sabrina left around 11:15pm. Mrs. Chisolm went to her bedroom. Pablo and Margret went to their room. Chrystal sat on a stool in the kitchen looking at her father and sister in law on the stairs. Tears ran from her cheek.

"Okay, you can go up to bed now. We will talk in the morning." Mr. Chisolm said as he helped Kaci up.

"Thanks dad. I love you." Kaci said hugging him and crying.

"I love you too. I am always here for you no matter what. And don't be afraid to call on me wherever I may be."

"I won't. Good night."

Kaci walked up the stairs as Mr. Chisolm looked at her and then walked towards his daughter and hugged her. Kaci entered the bedroom and closed the door. The lights were dimmed. She didn't see Dwayne and candles were lit. She frowned and went into the bathroom to have a shower. Dwayne was not in the bathroom. Kaci removed her clothes and stepped into the shower. Dwayne entered the bathroom. Kaci didn't see him. Dwayne stepped into the shower behind her. He gently touched her.

"What the…!" Kaci screamed.

"Don't worry it's just me." Dwayne smiled.

"What are you doing here?"

"I want to be with you. Do you remember when we would shower together when you would visit before we got married?"

"Yes I do."

“Can we please recreate those moments?”

“No.”

“Please Kaci, I am sorry. I really want to make it up with you.”

“Dwayne please just leave me alone.”

“See I am turned on just for you. Look at what you just caused.” Dwayne smiled pulling Kaci closer to him.

“Dwayne stop! Latoya did that too.” Kaci said hiding her smile.

“I know you want me as bad as I want you.” Dwayne said putting her nipple into his mouth.

“Oooooooh Dwayne stop!”

“See you are turned on too.”

Kaci pulled away and stepped from the shower. She dried with a towel as Dwayne sat on the bathtub looking at her. She slipped into her robe and walked from the bathroom. Dwayne smiled. Kaci sat on the bed and opened a gift box which had her name on it. She removed a necklace with Dwayne’s initial. She smiled and opened a gift bag and removed a cologne set along with a jewelry set and a rose.

She held the necklace. Dwayne stood at the bathroom door watching her. Kaci placed the gifts on the dresser and walked towards Dwayne and gave him the necklace and turned around as she lifted her hair.

"You like it?" Dwayne asked as he fastened the necklace.

"Yes I do. It's cute." Kaci said softly.

"Kaci I am sorry. I know gifts cannot make it up to you but it's a start."

"What do you mean by a start?" Kaci asked facing him.

"I have other things in store for us." Dwayne said holding her shoulders.

"Like?"

"It's a surprise."

"Okay then. Anything you say."

"Does this mean I just got back my wife whom I got married to last year?"
"Not so fast but it's getting there, and I wouldn't say the wife you married last year because that wife didn't love you but this one does." Kaci said kissing Dwayne.

"Wow! That felt real." Dwayne said kissing her back.

"Because that just came from my heart. I love you Dwayne."

"I love you too Kaci-Ann."

"I am sorry. I am the cause for all of this."

"Stop blaming yourself."

"I can't. Because of me I almost lost you. I was giving up on you but someone special inspired me not to."

"Who is that special person?"

"Laci. I went to see her today and I begged my mom forgiveness and also Laci." Kaci cried.

"You saw your sister! That's great baby! You deserve a medal for this!"

"I got my medal already."

"Really? Where is it?"

"He is standing in front of me. You are the best thing that has ever happened to me and I am so sorry I took so long to see that I had a prize right in front of me all along. I was just focused on my materialistic life that I didn't even see you slipping away. I am sorry and I don't know how I am going to make it up to you ever. You don't deserve a girl like me, you deserve better."

"Sssssshhhh… Don't say that. I knew I found the girl of my dreams the first day I saw you. I fell in love with you instantly. I caused that entire spilling of Sundae on your blouse to happen."

"What? How?"

"I kept on seeing you but I didn't want to approach you. I know you always visited that mall so I paid my friend to bump into you and then I come to your rescue and it worked."

"I should have known."

"Naaah, tonight is the night you should know."

"Oooooooh Dwayne. You are so sweet. I love you."

"I love you too. And I love our little munchkin down here." Dwayne said kissing her tummy.

Dwayne lifted her up and walked over towards the bed. Kaci screamed and giggled. Chrystal smiled as she laid on her bed hearing them. Dwayne opened her robe and began to caress her body as he removed the robe and his boxers. Dwayne began playing with Kaci's nipples as she placed wet kisses on his body. She began moan and groan and scream. Mrs. Chisolm overheard and began to smile.

"What's so funny?" Mr. Chisolm asked coming from the bathroom.

"I just heard my daughter in law screaming in pleasure. I am happy they are making it up. And I am sure Chrystal is listen to every groan." Mrs. Chisolm laughed.

"So do you want me to block your mind from all those sounds?"

"I thought you wouldn't ask. It's been over six months. It's long overdue."

"Come to papa!"

"Peter, where are you?" Chrystal asked.

"I am home. Where else would you expect me to be?" Peter asked.

"I am coming over. I cannot fucking take this anymore."

"CC, what's wrong? So late? Are you okay?"

"No! I am so not okay. My brother is fucking his wife and she is groaning with pleasure and my parents just started. I am trapped in the middle and I am sure that Pablo and Margret are doing the same downstairs."

"Okay, come on over. Somebody sounds jealous."

"I am not jealous. I just want to sleep."

"And you expect me to believe that?"

"Peter! Just stop!"

"I have to tell mom this!"

"If you ever! I promise I'll kill you and cover it up."

"Hurry and come on over. I am getting the bed warm for you. How many condoms should I get out for you?"

"We will decide that when I get there."

"I got you! You didn't want sex a minute ago."

"Peter!"

Chrystal got out of bed in her pajamas and left the house.

CHAPTER 28

"Good morning baby." Dwayne said kissing Kaci.

"Good morning, Mr. Chisolm." Kaci smiled kissing Dwayne.

"I got a title to my name."

"You deserved it. I seriously cannot move."

"Why? How comes?"

"You really expect me to answer you? You already knew what you did."

"Me? I did nothing. What do you want for breakfast?"

"Grapes."

"Kaci, you cannot just feed on grapes."

"That's what I want."

"I'll be back."

Dwayne got out of bed and got on his robe and went downstairs. It was now 9:05am. Mrs. Chisolm was in the kitchen searching the cupboard and Mr. Chisolm went to play golf.

"Good morning mother. Margret I want scrambled eggs and toast and a coffee. Fix something light for Kaci with grapes." Dwayne said

"Good morning son, where is Kaci?" Mrs. Chisolm smiled.

"She is upstairs." Dwayne smiled as he knew what his mother was up to.

"So isn't she coming down? It's Saturday."

"We know it's Saturday and no she isn't coming down."

"What did you do to the poor girl?"

"Mom! I did nothing to her."

"Okay then anything you say."

"Morning everybody!" Chrystal said entering the house.

"Where are you coming from?" Mrs. Chisolm asked.

"Peter's home! Dwayne was killing Kaci with whatever he has in his pants last night and she was groaning the fuck away. And I heard you and dad too but Kaci was louder so left! I wanted a peace of mind. Where is Kaci by the way?"

"She's is upstairs." Dwayne said.

"I want to see her."

"No! She is naked! You can see her later!"

"You guys aren't finished? But we had plans today!"

"I would suggest you cancel it! Because I have Kaci under house arrest today!"

"Oh my fucking God!" Chrystal shouted storming to her bedroom.

Around 3:30pm, Kaci and Dwayne came from the bathroom. Kaci got dressed in a pair of white high-waist pants, a short yellow chemise blouse and a pair of yellow flat shoes. She got on her jewelries and applied her makeup. She arranged a yellow t-shirt, a pair of white jeans pants and a pair of yellow Dessert Clarks for Dwayne. She took up her white handbag and Dwayne got on his white cap and they left the room together. Mrs. Chisolm had just arrived and saw them. She smiled. Chrystal was on the phone and she dropped her phone when she saw them. Pablo and Margret looked at them in awe. They stopped on the stairs as

Kaci placed Dwayne's earrings in his ears. Chrystal captured several photos of them.

"Hey mom. Hi CC." Kaci smiled as went into the kitchen to get grapes.

"You guys look awesome. I have always dreamed of seeing this day." Mrs. Chisolm smiled.

"Thank you and you will be seeing a lot more of it." Kaci laughed eating grape.

"Bro, you both are the best! So where are you both going?" Chrystal asked.

"Well I am getting her a phone. Then we are going by her parents, her father called for her and then I am taking my wife out on a date." Dwayne said kissing Kaci.

"Have fun and I hope you continue to date your wife." Mrs. Chisolm said.

"I will."

"I will ensure that he does all the time." Kaci laughed hugging Dwayne around his waist as they walked from the house.

They got in Dwayne's car and left. There was a love song playing.

"Babe?" Dwayne said.

"Yes…" Kaci answered.

"What kind of phone do you want this time?"

"An S8."

"No IPhone?"

"No. Not at this moment."

"Okay. I have a surprise for you later."

"Do you mind giving me a sneak peek?"

"I can just give you a kiss." Dwayne smiled quickly kissing her.

"That's not fair!"

"Why? What's wrong with my kisses?"

"That kiss won't tell me anything."

"Well that kiss will let you kiss me more."

"Are you sure about that?"

"Yes I am."

"Okay fine by me."

"I love you."

"I love you too."

Dwayne parked in the parking lot of Hill Country Galleria in Lakeway. They entered the Mall holding hands and went into AT&T. They were looking at phones and headsets. Dwayne purchased the phone for Kaci and then took her into Amy's Ice Creams. While he went to purchase the ice-cream, Kaci was talking to friend.

"I had no idea you got married. Who is the lucky guy?" The girl asked.

"He's right over there in the yellow shirt." Kaci smiled as she scrolled her phone.

"You mean the one with the girl hugging him?"

"What?"

"Yea, that's him right? He is the only guy I see in a yellow shirt."

"Excuse me, just a second."
Kaci walked off as her friend looked on.

"I want strawberry?" Latoya said rubbing Dwayne in his back.

"Babe, are you sure? You don't like strawberry. Or is the pregnancy working on your hormones already?" Dwayne asked as he was looking at the flavour board.

"Excuse Latoya, what the fuck are you doing here?" Kaci asked.

Dwayne turned around. He was shocked.

"Babes I am sorry. I didn't know it was her. I thought it was you. I thought you finished talking to your friend." Dwayne said.

"It's okay babe. I don't feel for ice-cream anymore. Let's go." Kaci said holding on to Dwayne and pulling him away.

Latoya stood looking them as Kaci introduced Dwayne to her friend. They left.

"Babe?" Dwayne said as he drove.

"Yes Dwayne?" Kaci answered as she set her phone.

"I am sorry."

"Babe, I said it's okay. I trust you okay. Now stop worrying yourself."

"Okay baby." Dwayne said as Kaci snapped a photo of them.

"How does this look?"

"I love it. Our first selfie together."

"I am posting it now. 'My Husband and I. Cute Aren't We?'"

After half an hour, they arrived at Kaci's old home in Dripping Springs. Dwayne came out and opened the door for Kaci. She came out and closed the door. They went to the door, Dwayne rang the doorbell. Laci opened the door.

"Kaci!" Laci screamed hugging her.

"Hey sister! How are you?" Kaci screamed.

"I am fantastic! I didn't know you were coming here! Come in! Hi Dwayne!" Laci smiled hugging Dwayne.

"Hey, how are you feeling?" Dwayne asked as he gave her a box of chocolates.

"I am great. You guys together! This is awesome! Mom! Guess who is here?" Laci shouted running to the kitchen.

"Who is there?" Mona asked.

"Come and see!"

Kaci was walking around the living room showing Dwayne some photos and some medals she received in school. Dwayne had his hand around her waist.

"This one was when Laci and I both had our first training on the bicycle." Kaci laughed.

"You guys are really dirty. But it's good to have memories." Dwayne laughed as he kissed her.

"Kaci and Dwayne?" Mona called.

"Hey mom." Kaci smiled hugging her mother.

"Hey mom." Dwayne said hugging Mona.

"It's a surprise to see you both here and happy too."

"Mom, so you guys didn't know we were coming?" Kaci asked.

"No, we didn't." Laci answered.

"But Mr. Robinson called last night and spoke to me for some time and he said we should come over today." Dwayne said.

"So you were the one he was talking to. I was wondering." Mona laughed.

"So where is dad?" Kaci asked.

"He went out with a friend. He'll be back soon though."

"Okay."

"Kaci?" Damion called as he entered the living room.

There was a tension in the room.

"Damion?" Kaci called back.

"What are you doing here?"

"I am sorry Damion, I really am. I know I am the worst sister you could have but I really want you to forgive me. I messed up and I…" Kaci started crying.

"I forgive you sis." Damion interrupted Kaci as he hugged her tightly.

"I am sorry."

"Listen I love you. I was just surprised to see you with your husband here. I was anticipating this day. Laci told me everything that happened yesterday. But I didn't expect to see you so soon especially with your husband after the incident I heard."

"I just took a table turn and looked back and I realize that I was hurting everyone who loved me and that made me sad and angry. I deserted my family for seven months and I regret doing that. I pushed my husband away for seven months and I regret that also. I just hope you all find it in your hearts to forgive me.”

“Kaci, I told you yesterday that I forgave you. A mother cannot go on if she can’t find it in her heart to forgive her child.” Mona said hugging her.

“We forgive you.” Damion said.

“I just hope dad will find it in his heart to forgive me because dad is a hard nut to crack. I know he will think it hard to forgive me. I just wish my daddy would forgive me.” Kaci cried.

“Come here Princess.” Patrick said as everyone looked at him surprising.

Kaci looked at him and wiped her tears. She smiled. She walked towards him. She hugged her father and he lifted her from the ground.

“Do I need to say anything?” Patrick asked.

“No daddy. Once I hear the word princess I know what it means.” Kaci laughed.

“You have gotten heavy.”

“I am not the same little girl anymore dad. I am twenty-one going twenty-two.”

“Guys, dinner is served.” Mona interrupted.

They sat at the table. Kaci's mouth dropped open when she saw Pedro.

CHAPTER 29

"Pedro? What are you doing here?" Kaci asked.

"I once loved a girl but she didn't love but I decided that if I love the sister then I could have her close to me as a sister in law." Pedro smiled.

"I know that you arc dating my sistcr but what arc you doing hcrc?"

"I wanted to visit my girlfriend."

"But the Pedro I know never ever wanted to leave Puerto Rico."

"Things have changed."

"So I see."

Pedro looked at Laci and then at Patrick who shook his head. Kaci found it weird. Pedro held Laci's hand. Shelly and Tawney looked at them. Laci was smiling.

"Laci, I love you and I cherish the six months that we have been together. You are an amazing girl and I love every moment I spend with you. I thought I was going to lose you but God knew I would be sad without you." Pedro started.

"Pedro, I know. This is not the place for this. Everyone's hungry." Laci said.

"Let him speak! We will listen!" Kaci smiled as everyone agreed.

"Laci you are my sunshine, my rain drops and the gentle wind that soothes my face. I can't imagine my life without you. You are my rainbow and I love you." Pedro continued.

"I love you too." Laci said kissing him, just as her father pushed a cup in front of her.

Everyone looked at him but he only shrugged. Laci looked in the cup and screamed.

"Yes! I'll marry you!" Laci screamed.

Kaci took the cup and looked in it and smiled. The cup was passed around the table as Pedro slipped the ring on Laci's finger. Every one began to eat except for Kaci. They were all laughing and commending Patrick and Pedro on their plan. Laci looked at Kaci and realized that she wasn't eating.

"Kaci, what's wrong?? Laci asked as everyone looked at her.

"Nothing. I just don't feel to eat." Kaci replied.

"Why what's wrong?"

"It's nothing. Enjoy your meal everyone I am okay." Kaci said as Dwayne rubbed her leg.

"Kaci, what is the matter? Are you sick?" Mona asked.

"Actually…" Kaci started as Dwayne held her hand and smiled.

"Actually what?"

"Dwayne and I are expecting our first child."

"Wow! That is awesome!" Laci exclaimed as she got up and hugged her.

"That's wonderful honey!" Mona exclaimed.

"Congrats guys." Shelly smiled.

"Congratulations!" Patrick said.

"Dwayne my man congrats!" Damion laughed as he knocked Dwayne's fist.

"Congratulations to you both." Pedro said.

"So you mean to tell me that during all of this chaos and you wanting to divorce her and you wanting to commit suicide, you both were expecting a child? Congratulations anyways. You guys are something else." Tawney said.

"So what do you want to eat?" Laci asked.

"Grape." Dwayne said as everyone laughed.

"But we are out of grapes."

"I bought some for her. It's in the car."

"I want some fresh air. I'll go for it." Kaci said.

"I'll come with you." Laci said.

The two girls went outside. They talked and talked and talked. When it was 6:04pm, Dwayne came out front with the rest of family. They bid their goodbyes and left.

"Babe, I enjoyed your family today." Dwayne said as they drove.

"I am glad you did." Kaci smiled as she ate her grapes.

"Now it's time for your surprise."

"Aren't you going to give me a clue?"

"No, Kaci."

"If you love me, you will."

"Kaci I love you but you are not going to bribe me into telling you."

“It’s not fair.”

“Kaci, please be quiet.”

“Fine!”

“Kaci?”

Kaci didn’t answer. Dwayne shook his head and continued driving.

CHAPTER 30

He parked in a parking lot near to the Don Mario Mexican Restaurant in Lakeway. He came out of the car and opened the door for Kaci who still wasn't speaking to him. Dwayne smiled.

"Kaci?" Dwayne called.

She looked at him.

"Kaci you can speak. Please?"

She was still silent.

"Kaci, come on."

"Fine. Where are we?" Kaci asked breaking her silence.

"Come on. You will find out soon."

Dwayne closed the door and held Kaci's hand. They crossed the road. Dwayne covered her eyes and led her to the building. The attendant opened the door.

"I made a reservation for two. Dwayne Chisolm." Dwayne said.

"Okay Mr. Chisolm, come this way." The attendant smiled as he led them to a table.

"Thank you." Dwayne said allowing Kaci to sit before removing his hands.

"Dwayne, where is this place?" Kaci asked looking puzzled.

"This is my surprise. Just guess where you are?"

"I don't know."

"Good night Mr. Chisolm, thank you for making it to Don Mario Mexican Restaurant, here are your menus. I'll be back to take your order." The waitress said handing them the menu before walking away.

"Are you serious? You remembered?" Kaci exclaimed.

"Yes I remembered. You are always talking about coming to this place so I decided to take you."

"You are going to make me cry."

"Please don't."

"What should I order?"

"Anything baby. I am not a fan of Mexican cuisine."

"Are you ready to place your order?" The waitress smiled with her notepad and pen.

"Yes please, I'll have a Ceviche, a small Menudo, Soft Tacos chicken with salsa the red hot flavour and a Mexican soda grape. Thank you." Kaci ordered.

"And you Mr. Chisolm?"

"I'll have a Guacamole, a small Pozole, a De La Casa, a Fish Taco, an Iced Tea." Dwayne ordered.

"No dessert?"

"Baby what would you like?"

"Omg. Homemade Flan!" Kaci smiled.

"Okay, your appetizer will be served in two minutes."

"Okay. Baby how are you feeling?"

"Great. Thank you. How are you going to manage all those spicy food?"

"I have to try and please my baby. It's your culture."

"You didn't have to."

"I wanted to."

Their appetizers were served. They ate and talked until around 8:30pm.

"Babe, I cannot eat that dessert." Kaci said.

"Okay we can take it home." Dwayne smiled.

"Okay. I enjoyed the night."

"It is not over yet."

"What?"

"You heard me. Waitress!"

"Yes sir." The waitress responded as she stood beside the table.

"We are taking this home. And can I have the bill please?"

"Okay sir, give me a minute. Darling! Get the bill for Mr. Chisolm please?" the waitress said.

Kaci sat on Dwayne's lap and kissed him.

"Babe, your tongue is spicy." Dwayne smiled.

"Too spicy for you?" Kaci laughed.

"As much as I would like to say no, yes."

"You are such a baby."

Here is the bill and this your bag." The waitress said.

"Thank you." Dwayne said taking the bill. "Okay, fifty-five bucks, here is seventy-five the change is yours." He continued as he gave her the money.

"Thank you sir and thank you Madame. We appreciate you dining here. Please come again." The waitress smiled.

"We will." Kaci smiled and looked at Dwayne.

Dwayne held the door and Kaci went out followed by him. She walked towards the car when Dwayne grabbed her and pulled her towards him. They started to kiss.

"Excuse can I take a picture of you? It's only a dollar?" A little boy asked.

"Sure." Dwayne said.

The little boy snapped the photo and gave them the printed version.

"Here is fifty dollars. It's all yours." Dwayne said.

"Really sir?"

“Yes. Take it all.”

“Thank you sir.”

“What’s next?” Kaci asked looking up at Dwayne.

“We are going to walk down there.”

“Walk to where?”

“You will see.”

CHAPTER 31

They walked for five minutes before entering Jules Tavern Night Club. Upon entering they heard 'Options' by Pitbull featuring Steven Marley and Dwayne began to sing it to Kaci. She began to blush. They went to the bar and sat on the stool. Dwayne ordered a drink and Kaci took a water. Afterwards they went to dance.

"I love this song! Omg!" Kaci screamed.

The songs that were playing were playlists from a Jamaican artiste named Ioctane.

Dwayne laughed as she sang the songs. They met up with some friends and they all enjoyed themselves. The song selections were based on Jamaican Dancehall and the patrons loved them. Dwayne was drinking hard even though Kaci told him not to. When they left the club it was 12:06am. They walked back to their car. Kaci drove home.

Just as Kaci parked she saw Mr. and Mrs. Chisolm entering the house around 12:47am. They entered the house shortly.

"Kaci, you guys are just coming in?" Mrs. Chisolm smiled.

"Yes, but I can see that you guys are just coming in." Kaci smiled as she placed the dessert in the refrigerator.

"Well yes, we went to my friends' engagement party. I can bet CC is dead asleep by now." Mrs. Chisolm said just as they heard the door opening.

It was Chrystal and she was dead drunk. She had her shoes in her hands.

"CC! You didn't drive in this condition?" Mrs. Chisolm asked as Kaci held her.

"Nooooooo! Bridgette has my car. I want to sleep."

Dwayne took her to her bedroom. Kaci went to her bedroom. Mrs. Chisolm went to her bedroom also. Dwayne closed the door and looked at Kaci who was taking off her jewelries. He went behind her and hugged her. They started to kiss as they stripped each other of their clothing and went into the shower.

 On the Monday morning, Kaci got dressed in pink blouse, a short black skirt and a pair of black flat shoes with her matching accessories and makeup and took up her pink handbag. Dwayne got dressed in a pink shirt, a pair of black pants and a pair of black shoes with a black and pink checkered tie.

Chrystal got dressed in a pair of black skinny jeans, a white blouse and a pair of black wedged shoes along with her small pink school bag.

Mrs. Chisolm got dressed in a black dress and a pair of yellow stilettos with her jewelries, makeup and a yellow handbag. Mr. Chisolm got dressed in a black pants suit with a white shirt and a pair of black shoes.

They met at the office. Dwayne and Kaci drove one car. The meeting was commenced and lasted for over two hours. All points were made and clarity was given where it was necessary. It was confirmed that Kaci would sit in as the receptionist until one was available. After the meeting Mrs. Chisolm left for her office and Chrystal left for school. Mr. Chisolm went to every department before he left.

"Sir, I am ordering lunch, should I order for you?" Kaci smiled over the phone.

"Yes babe. What are you ordering?" Dwayne smiled as he relaxed in his chair.

"I feel for chicken and chips."

"I want barbecue chicken with tofu."

"Okay. I'll send it when it arrives."

"I want you to bring it."

"Okay sir."

"Mrs. Chisolm, don't tell me you are talking to Mr. Chisolm like that?" Nicholas smiled as he leaned on the counter.

"He's my boss. Why not?" Kaci laughed.

"You are crazy."

"And Dwayne likes that."

"Anyways I want your signature on these. It's a transfer to the Golf Club."

"Oh okay. I totally forgot about this. How long will it take?"

"It's in the store room. So it can be transferred today if you like."

"Yes please. We need it badly. Let me call Christine and tell her to expect it."

"I like your smile."

"Thank you."

"Hey, watch how you are talking to my wife." Dwayne interrupted.

"Boss, I was just giving her a compliment. That's all." Nicholas smiled walking from the counter.

"Somebody sounds jealous." Kaci laughed as Dwayne held her hands and kissed them.

"Hey lovebirds." Laci interrupted.

"Hey baby girl." Dwayne said hugging her and kissing her on the cheeks.

"Hey sis! Hey Pedro!" Kaci smiled coming around the counter.

"I am just saying goodbye." Laci said hugging Kaci.

"No. you can't go." Kaci said.

"Kaci, I was supposed to be gone two months ago."

"But why do you have to go?"

"Because I made a commitment. Grandma is anticipating me and Pedro is depending on me."

"I am going to miss you." Kaci said hugging her sister tight.

"Mind the baby. I am going to miss you too. But I have to go. I will visit every chance I get."

"I will visit too. I think it's time I visit Puerto Rico. It's been years."

"See? I am getting you to visit your origin."

"Whatever."

"I love you."

"I love you too. Pedro take great care of my sister and don't let her cry because I will feel it and I will hurt you."

"She won't complain and you won't have to hurt me. She will be I n good hands."

Kaci and Laci hugged for ten minutes crying.

"Bye Kaci." Laci said walking away.

"Bye Laci." Kaci waved.

Kaci stood looking at them as they boarded the car and left.

"What you looking at?" Kaci asked Dwayne as she went around the counter.

"My prized possession." Dwayne smiled.

"Hello, good afternoon, I am ordering two lunches for Chisolm's Enterprise. Yes. I want a large Barbecue Chicken Leg and Thigh with Tofu and Salad. I also want a large Chicken and Chips the Breast. No I don't want any sauce. A Fruit Drink and a Grape Welch. Thank you. How much would that be? Okay no problem."

"How much is it?" Dwayne asked.

"Ten dollar fifty."

"Here."

"Thanks. Hey Christine, Kaci here. You are expect a package from Chisolm's Enterprise. Yes, it will be delivered any time before 4:00pm. I just signed the transfer sheet. And tell Garcia that I said she should price it and put in the system, mark them up ten percent. No! Tell him I said no! If he does he will be in big trouble with me and I won't be easy on him. Tell Garcia that when I stop by tomorrow the items should be in the gym in the showcase for sale. Really? Tell him to call me on my cellphone. Okay baby." Kaci spoke over the phone as Dwayne admired her.

"I just love looking at you when you talk."

"Whatever Dwayne. Don't you have work to do?"

"Can't I look at my wife?"

"I am your receptionist and I am your wife at home. Now go to your office."

"Only if you are coming with me."

"I am not coming up there."

Just then the lunches arrived and Dwayne ran upstairs.

"Dwayne!" Kaci hissed as she paid for the lunch.

"Thank you." the young man said leaving the office.

"Gawain, you oversee right here until I come back."

"Okay miss." The security answered.

Kaci went upstairs to Dwayne's office with his lunch.

"You think it's funny don't you?" Kaci said as Dwayne grabbed her and began to kiss her.

"Dwayne stop." Kaci said.

"Sssssshhhh…" Dwayne said closing the door.

"No! Just this one kiss and that's it. We just had a staff meeting about this behaviour in the office! No Dwayne! Right now I am getting a woman in her forties to be your receptionist!"

"Kaci you can't do that!"

"Watch me! You cannot be trusted with your receptionists so I am going to specify that we get a wait listen, we are getting a young man to be your receptionist and that's final!"

"Kaci! I don't want a man down there!"

"You will stay in your office and you won't flirt with the receptionist! Enjoy your lunch. Love you baby." Kaci said leaving the office.

Dwayne sat looking into space as he could not believe what Kaci had said. Kaci sat downstairs eating her lunch as she typed some documents. Just then a young man walked in with a bunch of flowers.

"Good afternoon, I would like to see Mrs. Kaci-Ann Chisolm." He said.

"This is her? How may I be of assistance to you?" Kaci asked.

"This is yours."

"Mine? Who gave you these?"

"I work with the florist and a gentleman called to order these roses for you. There is a card in there, which he had personalized for you. I'll take my leave now."

"Thank you."

Kaci read the note: '*To the most amazing wife ever. These roses aren't even a match to your beauty. I love you. Please change your mind about a male receptionist. Love Dwayne.*'

Kaci began to laugh. She placed the roses in a vase. Dwayne called her.

"Yes sir?" Kaci answered.

"Do you like them?" Dwayne asked.

"Yes I love them. They are wonderful and sweet."

"So?"

"I am still not changing my mind. Mathew, come here."

"Yes Miss?" Mathew answered walking towards her cowardly.

"What are the rules of this organization?"

"Why are you asking me that?"

"Mathew don't play smart with me. I am sure you were in the meeting this morning and the rules were enforced and your boss Mr. Dwight Chisolm told us not to be lenient on you guys. This is a no smoking zone and you are on duty by the way. Why were you smoking here?"

“I am sorry.”

“Hon, is that Mathew Chambers?” Dwayne asked.

“Yes it’s him.”

“Send him to my office please. I am tired to talk to him about that. I have to take actions now.”

“Okay, Mr. Chisolm wants to see you in his office now.”

“But Miss. Please?”

“I don’t make the rules. I only enforce them. He is waiting on you.” Kaci smiled as she continued typing.

“Sir, you wanted to see me?” Mathew said knocking the door.

“Yes, come in. have a seat.” Dwayne said looking upset.

Dwayne stood looking out the window with his hands in his pocket. Mathew sat looking tense.

“You have a family to feed right?” Dwayne asked.

“Yes sir. My wife and three children.” Mathew answered.

"Did you know that jobs are hard to find here in Texas?"

"Yes sir."

"How long have you been working here?"

"Four years sir."

"How many times have I spoken to you about smoking in the office? Threatening employees? Assaulting the female employees?"

"Quite a lot sir."

"What were my exact words when I caught you smoking in the container last week?"

"You said that 'I will not spare you another chance because you are getting out of hand. And you need to be placed back in line'."

"Mathew, give me the name of at least one organization that would have given you all the chances I did."

"I don't know of any sir."

"Hmmmm, Nicholas print document fourteen and address it to Mathew Chambers. I need it ASAP!" Dwayne said over the phone.

"Sir please, give me another chance. Please I beg of you. My wife is not working and her mother is ill. My daughter is starting high school next week and I have a young baby. Sir please, I promise I won't do it again. Please sir? Please? I have mortgage and bills to pay sir. Please sir?" Mathew cried.

"Why didn't think about all of those while I kept giving you chances? This is the last straw."

"Sir? Please I beg of you? Sir, you have a family I am sure you wouldn't want someone to do this to do."
"I am different from you. I don't work for anyone but you work for me and I have rules."

"Sir, here is the document." Nicholas said as he knocked and entered the office.

"Give it to him. Nick inform Natalie that she will be in charge of Mathew's post for three weeks." Dwayne said as Nicholas left the office.

"Sir you can't do this." Mathew begged.

"In that letter it is stating that you are officially on three weeks suspension starting now without pay. You should return to work on the fourteenth of August at 9:00am and you report to my office first thing. You may go now." Dwayne said as he walked into the bathroom.

Mathew left the office. After collecting his bag he went downstairs. He looked at Kaci.

"Mathew?" Kaci called.

"Yes?" Mathew answered.

"What happened up there?"

"I got suspension for three weeks."

"Sorry to hear. If I knew you were on watch I wouldn't have said anything to you."

"That's okay. You were just doing your job. After all he is your husband."

"I hope you learn your fucking lesson!"

Mathew walked from the office.

CHAPTER 32

Three days after, Kaci was in office when two young ladies and a gentleman walked in. she spoke to them and they sat in the waiting area. Four minutes later two ladies and two gentlemen walked in. Kaci handed them some forms and they began filling them out.

"Keisha, come here please?" Kaci said over the phone.

She was sending an email and making a phone call when Keisha came to her desk.

"Hold on Christine, Keisha take these seven visitors to the conference room please. They should be finished with these forms, so you can collect them. Hand them the tests papers, ensure that they aren't too clustered. You can oversee them. By the way were you busy?" Kaci smiled.

"Not really, I was putting some letters in an envelope." Keisha responded.

"You can take them with you. I'll be up as soon as Chrystal is here."

"Okay miss. Ladies and gentlemen come with me please." Keisha said walking up the passage.

"Christine I am back. Set up that meeting for tomorrow. No I have to be there. She is out of place so inform her that she should be present in my office tomorrow morning at 8:00am sharp. Okay sweetie." Kaci spoke before ending the call.

"I am stressed!" Chrystal shouted as she entered the office.

"What's wrong with you?" Kaci smiled.

"You're smiling? School is stressing me out and then my chief model called me to inform me that she wants a raise to model my swim wears or she quits! To heck with her!"

"So why don't you just give her a raise?"

"Kaci, she got a raise last month! No one else in America is paying their chief model US$2000 per fortnight. It's either a thousand bucks or less! Anyways let's go get these interviews because I have an exam at 1:30pm and it a quarter to twelve now."

Both girls went upstairs and conducted the interviews. They educated the group about the company and what it does. They informed them of their role as being a receptionist also. Afterwards they interviewed each individual personally. After interviewing, they came to a decision and smiled.

"Ladies and gentlemen, I am grateful that you all could have made it today. We appreciate it but as you all know that we are only open to one position at this moment and so we have to choose only one person even though you all have the qualities that we are looking for, we still had to choose one." Kaci smiled.

"Okay, Donovan Green, Amy Weathers, Dion Grey, Gregory Williams, Joseph White and Keith Brown, we are sorry. We will be looking forward to working with you in the future. Angel Bradford, step over here please. The rest of you may leave." Chrystal smiled.

"Thank you so much. I won't let you guys down." Angel smiled as she shook Kaci and Chrystal's hands.

"Welcome aboard. CC, it's 1:15pm. Angel let's go meet your boss whom you will be seeing every day and then I'll give you a tour around the office." Kaci smiled.

They walked out of the conference room and down the passage to Dwayne's office. Kaci knocked and entered.

"Hey baby." Dwayne smiled.

"Hey sweetheart. I am introducing your receptionist to you. She will start tomorrow. Her name is Angel Bradford." Kaci smiled.

"Hey, welcome aboard, Angel. I am Dwayne Chisolm. I hope you will be with us for a long time and that you will enjoy your stay." Dwayne said looking directly into Angel's eyes and shaking her hand.

"Thank you sir. Is she your wife?" Angel asked.

"Yes she is."

"Angel do have children?"

"Why sir?"

"No don't take this the wrong way. From time to time different employees are chosen to go on business trips and so on. I wouldn't want to take you away from your children if you have."

"Oh okay. If that's the case, no not as yet but hopefully after I get married, I will adopt maybe two."

"Adopt? But why?"

Kaci began to smile.

"I won't be able to reproduce and I love children so my fiancé said we could adopt because she loves children also."

"She?"

"Yes, I am a lesbian."

"Lesbian? But why? A nice young lady like you?"

"I hate men. I have been a lesbian since I was like thirteen and I am twenty- three now. I have never looked at a man before and I don't intend to. My fiancé is jealous."

"That's enough of her business now. Angel let's go." Kaci interrupted as Dwayne grabbed her arm.

"Why Kaci?" Dwayne asked as Angel stepped outside.

"Dwayne, you seem hurt. Why? She is just an employee."
"I know but why a lesbian?"

"Because I don't trust you around your receptionist Dwayne. And by the way it was CC's idea. I love you."

Dwayne hissed his teeth and Kaci left the office.

"Angel, this is Nicholas, he is your boss' assistant. Whenever Dwayne is out, he is in charge. Nicholas this is Angel our new receptionist."

"Welcome aboard, Angel." Nicholas said shaking her hand and looking into her eyes.

"Thank you. Excuse me, not to be rude, I don't like how you are looking at me." Angel smiled.

"But why?"

"She is a lesbian. She doesn't like men, moving right along."

"Thank you. I so hate men. You are cute though. I like you." Angel smiled.

"Uhmmm, we do not condone staff fraternization of any kind in the office okay. And most if not all of the females here are heterosexuals so I would advise you to just keep it business; I don't want them to feel uncomfortable. This is the break room (Kaci's cellphone began ringing) Keisha finish giving her a tour please? I have to take this. Angel come downstairs to me when you are finish okay? Hey sis?" Kaci said walking off.

"Kaci, guess what?" Laci asked on the phone.

"What? You are pregnant?"

"Kaci? No I am not pregnant! I got the pass!"

"Are you serious?"

“Yes I am serious! But it’s only one master suite available for now. The others are booked up until February.”

“Okay do one thing, book the room. We will be there on Saturday.”

“Kaci, have you spoken to Dwayne about this?”
“Nope! But we will be there!”

“Okay. Will you be paying by cash or card?”

“I’ll be using my card. Later. Dwayne?” Kaci said entering the office and giving him a massage.

“Kaci, what did I do to deserve this?” Dwayne asked.

“Nothing. I just love you that’s why.”

“But you were the one who said we shouldn’t do this at work.”
“I know baby, but we can bend the rules.”

“Kaci what do you want?”

“Nothing, can’t I give my husband a massage again? Or do you want me to go in a mood that you won’t like?”
“Kaci what do you want?”

“We are going to Puerto Rico on Saturday for a month.”

“What?”

“You have to. Laci already booked our rooms. I want to go for my birthday. Don’t you want me to be happy baby?”

“Kaci, I would go but I have a hectic week ahead of me!”

“No you don’t.”

“What do you mean by?”

“I already moved your meetings to a month and Nicholas already handled two of the meetings you had for next week and according to your schedule you are free. And don’t mention your mother’s bidding party because Chrystal found your replacement already. Your father is not leaving until next year so he decided to come to office now and then. Please?’

“Fine! You win!”

“Puerto Rico here we come! I promise you I’ll give you the best tour ever!”

“I love you Kaci!”

“I love you too.”

They sealed their deal with a kiss…

THE END….

©2017 Tasheika Powell

www.ingramcontent.com/pod-product-compliance
Lightning Source LLC
Chambersburg PA
CBHW081513250726
48659CB00009B/2796